INVITATION TO DRAMA

INVITATION
TO
DRAMA

One Act Plays for Secondary Schools
selected and edited by

ANDREW A. ORR, M.A.

EDWARD ARNOLD

© The Macmillan Company of Canada 1962

This anthology was first published in 1956 by
the Macmillan Co. of Canada in the St. Martin's Classics.
The present edition was first published by permission
in the *World of English* series in 1962 by
Edward Arnold (Publishers) Ltd
25 Hill Street, London W1X 8LL

Reprinted   1963, 1964, 1965, 1966, 1968,
               1971, 1972, 1974, 1976, 1979

057908

ISBN: 0 7131 1328 6

Printed in Singapore by Chong Moh Offset Printing Pte. Ltd.

PREFACE

This collection of plays was designed for use in the first forms of Canadian secondary schools. In the past five years it has been widely and successfully used in high schools in the Provinces of Ontario and Quebec. It is hoped that this British edition will find equal popularity in other parts of the Commonwealth with pupils in the first or second years of secondary education.

Two main objectives were kept in mind while choosing the material: the first was to provide plays of literary merit which would capture the interest of the young student and stimulate lively classroom discussion; the second was to gather together plays which reveal a sense of theatre, and which could be performed by the student player. Each play has proved its stage-worthiness in performance. *The Monkey's Paw, The Happy Journey*, and *Sunday Costs Five Pesos* have done so over the years. Variety too was sought, variety of period, setting, theme, style, and type. In all, the selection offers sufficient scope for the enterprising teacher to create interest in drama.

The one-act play has become a highly specialized form of dramatic writing. It may be compared to the short story which demands a skill quite different from that required in the writing of a novel. In both the shorter literary forms, the writer must say what he has to say quickly and boldly. Furthermore, the one-act play exhibits most of the dramatic elements evident in the full-length play, and therefore provides an excellent prelude to the study of more complicated dramas. By means of the one-act play the young student will become familiar with such terms as theme, plot, character, setting, and climax.

THEME. Just as the theme of a piece of music is the recurring melody, so the theme of a play is the recurring idea. It is the thread which binds the various incidents of the play together. For example, the theme of *The Pigeon with the Silver Foot* is that the romantic dreams of young people belong to no particular place or no definite time. The twentieth century English girls, Mary and Joanna, have the same hopes and dreams as Bianca and Mario who lived in Renaissance Italy. Every good play has such a dominant idea which a careful study of the words and actions of the characters will reveal.

PLOT. The theme is expressed through the plot and the characters. The plot of a one-act play must not be too complicated. A single incident should make up the story; there is no time to deal with supplementary incidents or sub-plots as they are called. Though there is normally only one scene in a one-act play, shorter divisions are occasionally introduced to indicate the passage of time or a change of place. *The Monkey's Paw* illustrates the conventional method of indicating the passing of time by dividing the play into scenes. *The Happy Journey, The Pigeon with the Silver Foot*, and *A Battle of Wits* reveal other methods of presenting plots which involve changes of location and which extend over longer periods of time.

At the beginning of every play (one-act or full-length) the author must give the audience sufficient information to enable it to understand the action which follows. This necessary explanation is known as the *exposition*. In a full-length play, the playwright may spend most of the first act doing this, but in a one-act play, this is not possible. As a result, every speech and every action must have a purpose; no words may be wasted.

When he has given the audience all the required information about the events and the people, the writer proceeds to introduce a new fact or a new character which changes the situation and stirs the interest. This makes the action more complex and is, therefore, known as the *complication*. He continues adding surprise to surprise until his story reaches its climax.

The *climax* in a play is the high point of the action. This high point occurs in a dramatic play when the conflict becomes most intense, and in a comedy or farce when the confusion becomes most hilarious or ridiculous. After this point, the problem presented in the first part of the play is solved. Sometimes, in a one-act play the climax comes right at the end and any further explanation is unnecessary; at other times it is reached before the end, and the play has a quieter close. You will find examples of both types in this book.

CHARACTER. Because a one-act play lasts approximately thirty minutes, there is little opportunity for the development of character. The author has no time to show how the character changes with age or with changing circumstances. If we were to watch an artist paint a portrait, we would see the picture grow stroke by stroke. Such a growth we can also observe in the building up of a character in a novel or a long play, but in a one-act play, the process is similar to the unveiling of the finished portrait: the characters are quickly revealed to us.

In studying the one-act play, it is interesting to note how the writer goes about his task. Here are a number of questions which will help us to discover the artistry and meaning of the play. Does the play have a theme? What is the theme? How does the writer introduce it? How does he establish, at the beginning of the play, the relationship among the characters? Do we learn more about the characters from what they do than from what they say? Does the speech of the characters seem to be natural or artificial? What complications which delight and surprise the audience does the writer introduce? How does he prepare for the climax? What point is the climax? If the climax does not come at the end of the play, how does he sustain interest after it has passed? How long is the action of the play supposed to last? If it is to extend over a longer period of time than the duration of the performance, how does the author indicate the passage of time? How important to the plot is the setting? How would interest in the play be increased by a stage presentation? Is the author attempting to teach a lesson, or merely to entertain? If the former, what lesson does he wish to teach? Does he succeed in making the lesson interesting by the manner in which he presents it? Does the play have a satisfactory ending?

We must enjoy what we read and see, and most of our reading and viewing is directed towards that end. By trying to find the answers to the suggested questions, we increase our enjoyment. But we should always remember that however interesting a play may be to read and analyse, it never truly becomes a play until it is performed. All of the plays in this book can be performed by young players. Not all are easy, but all are rewarding.

A number of references, and some of the vocabulary of *The Happy Journey* will be unfamiliar to a reader who is not American. The following explanations may help.

page 179: *aggie*—marble.

page 187: *speak-easies*—saloons which illegally sold alcoholic beverages during the period of prohibition.

page 188: *Knights of Columbus*—a Roman Catholic laymen's organization founded in New Haven, Connecticut, in 1882. Its purpose was to promote brotherhood and to further the interests of the Roman Catholic Church. When the garage attendant says he is 'Knights of Columbus', he merely means that he is a Roman Catholic, and does not frequent the Y.M.C.A.

page 189: *hot-dog*—a highly spiced sausage in a bun, garnished with mustard and relish.

page 190: *leather*—the tough skin of the sausage.

page 193: *A and P store*—The Atlantic and Pacific Store. A large chain store found in most parts of the North American Continent.

page 193: *kittycorner*—the diagonally opposite corner.

CONTENTS

INVITATION TO DRAMA

PEDLAR'S PROGRESS

by

NORA RATCLIFF

CHARACTERS

The Priest
Martha (his housekeeper)
Dickon (her son)
Piers (the village tailor)
Gill (his wife)
Meg ⎱
Lucy ⎰ (their daughters)

The Pedlar
Matthew (the Merchant)
Barbara (his wife)

The Landlord
Tib (his servant)

The Constable
Jakes (his assistant)

Crowd of villagers according to size of stage

SCENE: The Village

TIME: About 1450

PEDLAR'S PROGRESS

Scene: *An English village in the fifteenth century. Essential to the action are the exteriors, with practical doors, of a small cottage, stage right, and the village inn, stage left. At the centre back are the village stocks, set under the market cross or an old tree.*

In front of the inn is a rough wooden table, with benches or stools. Beside the PRIEST's *cottage on the right, two solitary flowers are growing. One is a gigantic sunflower, the bloom higher than the thatched roof of the cottage; the other is a hollyhock, not more than eighteen inches high.*

The curtain goes up on a morning of brilliant sunshine. TIB, *an adenoidal half-wit, is sitting at the table outside the inn busy with a bowl of paste. She will be busy with this paste throughout the play. She only speaks three times, but a lump of well-kneaded flour and water offers infinite pantomimic possibilities.*

The PRIEST *comes out of the cottage carrying a miniature green watering-can. He is a large, stout specimen of his order; a gentle, good-natured soul. He sets to work on his flowers, contentedly humming a Gregorian chant.*

After a few seconds, MARTHA, *his housekeeper, also comes out. She is tall, thin, and vixenish. She marches off-stage*

2

with her wooden bucket. There is a loud splash. She returns, bangs down her bucket in front of the doorway and stands, arms akimbo, glaring at the PRIEST.

MARTHA. So you're at it again.

PRIEST. There has been no rain for six weeks.

MARTHA. Is that any of your business?

PRIEST. The flowers need water. They——

MARTHA. If the good Lord wanted them to have water He'd send it. I don't hold with all this interfering with Nature.

PRIEST. But, Martha, man is often called upon to help——

MARTHA. If you want to help Nature on a bit, you'd better go and see to them bees. They're swarming. And don't forget to put something on your head.

PRIEST. You know I never do, and the bees never dream of harming me. (*He peers down at the hollyhock and carefully removes a caterpillar.*)

MARTHA. Well, are you going to 'em or not?

PRIEST. Yes, yes, of course. My little golden parishioners. (*He trots into the cottage, falling over the bucket as he goes.*) Tut—tut—tut.

> (MARTHA *looks up and down the village street to make sure nothing is happening without her knowledge. Then she settles down to a steady search of the doorstep and the ground in front of the cottage.* GILL, *the tailor's wife, comes in from the left. She is rather short and as stout as may be.*)

GILL. Ye look as if ye'd lost something, Martha.

MARTHA. Lost, is it? Here am I with my needle gone, and one more day without it and that lad o' mine'll need to stay in bed for shame of showing his skin.

GILL. He'll not mind that.

MARTHA. No more he will, but I shall. I've not bred him to be naught but a burden to me—the idle good-for-nothing.

GILL. And you think it's lost out here?

MARTHA. I've searched every inch inside. Clawing up the rushes I've been, like a cat making a bed for kittens. And never a sign of it.

GILL. Well, I'm not much use for looking, I'm not. Nigh blind as a bat, I am. (*She stoops and searches; her nose is indeed only a few inches off the ground.*)

MARTHA. The lout himself must help.

GILL. And I'll call my girls.

(GILL *moves up-stage and calls off left, whilst* MARTHA *shouts into the cottage.*)

MARTHA. Dickon! Dickon! Lazier than his father, though you'd scarce think it possible!

GILL. Meg! Lucy! Here! Come here, I say.

(DICKON, *a thin, lanky "natural", edges out of the cottage. When he sees the girls coming from the other side he tries to back away again.* MEG *and* LUCY *are young and rather pretty village girls, more or less of an age.*)

MARTHA. Nay, out you come! That needle's to be found before your breeches can be mended. Help look for it.

(DICKON *gazes round, up and down the walls of the cottage, taking great care not to stoop.* MEG *and* LUCY *hang back, giggling at the sight of* DICKON.)

GILL. You help, girls, you help! We can't see a neighbour in such trouble.

MEG. Help with what, Mother?

GILL. Help find her needle, of course.

LUCY. What, her needle gone?

MEG. Oh, dear. Poor Martha!

>   (*They are all set to work.* MARTHA *turns to* DICKON,
>   *who is still carefully erect.*)

MARTHA. What ails the lad? Do you think I've lost it on the thatch?

DICKON. Nay, Mother, you know I daren't bend to look for it till it's found. I had to stand to eat my breakfast.

>   (PIERS, *the tailor, comes in. He is a wizened little
>   fellow, with something of the humour-pathos of
>   Charlie Chaplin. His eyes are fixed on his objec-
>   tive,* MARTHA's *cottage, with the result that he
>   cannons into her stooping figure.*)

PIERS. Ah, there you are, gossip Martha! Now I was wondering, could you lend me such a thing as a needle——

MARTHA. Lend you my needle! What do you think we're all doing here but looking for my needle? Wasn't I about to send my Dickon across, for very shame's sake, to borrow your needle?

GILL. And pray what's happened to your own needle, husband?

PIERS. Why, I've just—— I've just——

GILL. Just what? Swallowed it, I'll be bound. Always sticking it between your teeth. Haven't I told you, time and time again——

PIERS. No, no, my angel. Not swallowed. I've broken it!

GILL.   Broken it, have you? As if that wasn't as bad! If ever a woman had to put up with a more senseless creature let me see her.

PIERS.   Faith, sweeting, I——

GILL.   Sweeting, indeed! And who's going to live on being called sweeting? And where's our bread to come from when you haven't the sense to look after your tools? Did I marry you to be starved to death and then called "sweeting"?

MARTHA   (*taking advantage of* GILL's *pause for breath*). And here we are, our clothes dropping off our backs and not a needle in the village. And me helped up with an idle, lazy, good-for-nothing——(*to* DICKON) And you stand here and never do a hand's turn for the mother that's toiled and slaved——

GILL   (*stalking her husband round the stage*). If you can't sew, then ye'd better get to a man's job straight away. There's plenty of wood ye can be chopping, and——

PIERS.   But, wife, have ye forgotten how my back ached the last time I chopped wood?

GILL   (*still in pursuit*). And there's the garden needs weeding and digging——

PIERS.   But wife, ye know the last time I digged the garden——

GILL.   No, I don't! It wasn't in my memory. And then there's water to fetch in, and——

PIERS   (*as his wife hurries him off*). Oh, would to heaven I could find a needle!

(*Exeunt* GILL *and* PIERS.)

PRIEST   (*appearing at door*). Martha! Martha, can ye come? There's great trouble in here, for the cat's upset the whole bowl of cream.

MARTHA. Was ever a poor woman worse beset? Fools and thieves indoors and out! (*to* DICKON) And you, you wastrel, hasten to fetch me them fagots, for it's no more food you'll get, stand or sit, till you've earned it!

> (MARTHA *follows the* PRIEST *into the cottage.* DICKON *is left alone with* MEG *and* LUCY. *He stands staring at them. They come up on either side of him.*)

MEG. You're not looking for your mother's needle. You'll never find it that way.

DICKON (*with a shy, but ecstatic wriggle*). I don't care.

LUCY. But it's a great pity she should have lost it.

DICKON. I don't care!

MEG. You'd better hurry and fetch the fagots as she bade you——

LUCY. Or else she'll scold you when she comes again.

DICKON (*almost hiccuping with the thrill of the conversation*). I—don't—care! (*The girls laugh.*)

LUCY. What do you care for, Dickon?

MEG. Do you care for us, Dickon?

LUCY. Me most, Dickon?

MEG. Or me, Dickon?

LUCY. You can't have us both, you know, Dickon.

MEG. You'll have to choose some day.

DICKON. There's no hurry 'at I know on.

LUCY. Oh, indeed. That's all you know, Master Dickon.

MEG. I wouldn't be too sure of either of us, if I were you.

> (PEDLAR'*s cry is heard, off-stage.*)

PEDLAR. What d'ye lack?

LUCY. O-oh, the pedlar! (*She runs back-stage and looks off to left.*)

MEG (*joining her*). A stranger. This one hasn't been here before.

LUCY. I hope he's got fine things to show us.

> (PEDLAR *strolls in from up-stage left. He is tall and good-looking; something of a mixture of Robin Hood and Mephistopheles.*)

PEDLAR. What d'ye lack? What d'ye lack? Ah—give you good-day, maidens. I've fine things here in my pack, will make your bright eyes shine the brighter.

MEG. Yes; but we've no money for them.

PEDLAR. And what about the pretty man who's with you? Surely, sir, you'll not be long in putting your hand in your pocket for two such beauties.

> (DICKON, MEG, *and* LUCY *examine the* PEDLAR'S *pack and chatter to him in the background.* MERCHANT MATTHEW *has entered down-stage left. He is old, bearded, and richly dressed. He sits on a stool by the table and calls impatiently.*)

MATTHEW. Landlord! Landlord! Fetch your master, girl.

> (TIB *begins a long struggle to clear her hands of paste. Finally she gives it up and runs to the door of the inn dangling them helplessly beside her.*)

TIB. Mester! Mester!

MATTHEW (*as she turns*). Where is your master?

TIB. I don't know.

> (*She settles down to her work again. Enter* LAND-LORD, *from inn. He is big and heavily built. He moves with exasperating deliberation.*)

LANDLORD. What's your will, sir?

MATTHEW. Ale, cheese, and bread. I must wait until my mare has a shoe righted at the blacksmith's.

LANDLORD (*speaking as slowly and deliberately as he moves*). If it's Hodge 'at's doing your job, sir, ye'll have time to eat us out of all the house afore he's finished. I tell you, sir, I've never known a slower man than Hodge. (*He picks up the jug and moves slowly to the door, where he turns.*) There isn't a slower man in all this village. (*After a solemn pause, as if considering the matter.*) Not in all this village there isn't—not slower than Hodge.

> (*He goes in. There is a burst of laughter from* MEG *and* LUCY.)

MEG (*to the* PEDLAR). Fie, fie, sir! You mustn't say such things!

LUCY. Come, Meg, if we do not get back to our spinning our mother will scold. (*She takes* MEG *by the hand.*)

MEG (*calling back as they run off left*). And what about those fagots, Dickon?

DICKON. I wish I could have bought them something. Have you nothing you could sell me for a groat, sir?

PEDLAR. Ay. I could sell you a deal of advice for that.

DICKON. But is it pretty? Would the girls like it?

PEDLAR. I'll not promise that. It's a commodity they've little use for.

DICKON. Then I'll not buy it. I'll buy naught but what the girls like. I'll go earn more money until I can buy 'em trinkets.

> (*He giggles and runs off right. The* PEDLAR *strolls down to* MATTHEW.)

PEDLAR. Well, what luck, brother? For though your pack be heavier, our game's the same—and so, we're brothers.

MATTHEW. Brother to a peddling Jack, indeed! That's a rare jest. And yet, there's one thing I'd buy off you, if I could.

PEDLAR. What's that, sir? There's nothing I won't sell you—at a price. What is it you lack?

MATTHEW. Your youth and looks; and the power to coax a laugh out of a pretty maiden. I've long since lost the trick of it.

PEDLAR. What? A girl's laugh is easy angled for.

MATTHEW. When you're young. They don't heed me now as they used to.

PEDLAR (to TIB, after looking cautiously round). Must you work here? (TIB nods.)

PEDLAR. Can ye work with your ears shut?
(TIB nods.)

PEDLAR. And keep your mouth shut after?
(TIB nods.)

MATTHEW. Why, what have you to say needs all this?

(PEDLAR is about to speak when the LANDLORD returns with jug. PEDLAR moves away a little.)

LANDLORD. That slow he is. It's well Hodge doesn't keep an inn. Ye'd be a day before ye got as much as a cup of ale. (He looks into the jug; there is a low, rumbling chuckle.) And here am I, that flurried and hurried and chased from pillar to post—would you believe it, sir—I've forgotten to put ale i' t' jug! (He chuckles again.) But, there, ye'll have time to drink this and half a dozen more afore Hodge'll have finished your mare. That slow he is—

and a bit—you know. (*He taps his head.*) Eh, the things that man forgets! (*To the* PEDLAR.) Will you be drinking too, sir?

PEDLAR.   Be sure I shall. And not out of an empty jug neither.

(LANDLORD *stumps slowly back into the inn.*)

MATTHEW.   Tell me, girl, is your master mad?

TIB.   I don't know.

(MATTHEW *shrugs his shoulders.* PEDLAR *laughs.*)

MATTHEW.   You had something to tell me, sir.

PEDLAR   (*crossing over to him*). I have. You said you wanted the days back when a maid laughed with you—not at you.

MATTHEW.   That's true.

PEDLAR.   Ye meant it?

MATTHEW.   What do you think!

PEDLAR   (*his eyes fixed on* MATTHEW). And if I was to tell you I could sell you the means of doing it?

MATTHEW.   Kind heaven, another madman.

PEDLAR   (*sitting on table and gazing hard at* MATTHEW). Do I look mad—or *queer*?

MATTHEW.   In truth you might be either—or both.

PEDLAR.   What would you give to have back your youth?

MATTHEW.   My youth? Nay, ye're jesting. You're——

PEDLAR   (*persisting; his face close to* MATTHEW'S). What would you give me for your youth?

MATTHEW.   Are you the Devil, then, in pedlar's guise?

PEDLAR.   Ye'd be wiser not to ask. Come, your bargain?

MATTHEW.   Youth? For how long?

PEDLAR.   Why, to prove my good faith I'll give you a sample of my wares first. Let's say, to start with, your youth till midnight. And then, if you're satisfied, we'll strike a longer bargain later.

MATTHEW. Your terms?

PEDLAR. Five—*ten* gold pieces, and your youth till midnight.

MATTHEW. Done! And after?

PEDLAR. Why, that'll be a harder bargain. But take what offers you first. Fetch your gold.

MATTHEW. Ye swear you can do this?

PEDLAR. Can you look me in the face and doubt it?

MATTHEW. N-no . . . there's something in your eyes— if you're not the Devil himself, you're his right-hand man.

PEDLAR. Hurry, then, with your gold.

MATTHEW. Ay, ay. My youth. (*He gets up to go and then turns back.*) But can you make sure I shall see the same two maids who laughed with you just now?

PEDLAR. That's easy. Fetch your gold, man.

MATTHEW. Ay, ay. He-he-he! My youth . . . And two maids waiting for me!

> (MATTHEW *goes out left, chuckling.* PEDLAR *sits on stool, thinking out his plans.* MARTHA *comes to cottage door to shake a duster.*)

MARTHA. Good-day to you, Pedlar.

PEDLAR (*moving over*). Good-day to you, Mistress. Is there aught you lack?

MARTHA. Ay, a deal more than you can ever sell me. And likely to go on lacking it, with naught but a scapegrace of a son who should be keeping me and not me him.

PEDLAR. The willing are always put on, gossip. That's the way the world goes.

MARTHA. Well, I, for one, don't mean it to go that way much longer. But I haven't come out here to stand and chatter. Now, have you in your pack a needle?

PEDLAR. In truth, you've asked for the one thing I haven't got. Ribbons, now, or laces——

> (*He makes to move over to his pack, which is still lying near the stocks.*)

MARTHA. I tell you I want naught but a needle. I've lost my own——

PEDLAR. Lost it? Dearie, dear, now, what a pity!

MARTHA. More pity that you call yourself a pedlar and can't keep things for a decent hussif, but only ribbons and laces for wantons.

PEDLAR. Now, I'll be passing this way to-morrow. I'll bring you one. And, maybe, if you were to pay me for it now, ye'd be surer of your needle.

MARTHA. And maybe if I wasn't to pay you I'd be surer of my money. Ye'll not see the colour of my money till the needle's in my hand.

> (MARTHA *shakes the duster in his face and goes in. The* PEDLAR *sneezes heavily, bringing his head nearly to his knees. From this position he sees the needle near the step, stoops, and picks it up. Holds it up to show* TIB, *laughs, and puts his fingers to his lips. He moves back-stage. Looks off, sees someone and beckons.* PIERS *trots in.*)

PIERS. What, Mac! Art thou back in these parts!

PEDLAR. Hush, man! No names, no gibbets. Faith, though, I've a rare job for thee, Piers.

PIERS. Nay, the last job I did for thee——

(*He begins to move off, but the* PEDLAR *drags him back.*)

PEDLAR.   Let it go, man. What's done is done. Think no more of it. This time thou shalt share in the profits as well as in the jest.

PIERS.   I trust it's a better job than chopping wood. My back's near broken, and look ye here, my finger's nigh off, where the axe slipped.

PEDLAR (*bringing him down-stage*). There's money in this job.

PIERS.   Ay?

PEDLAR.   There'll soon come along a grey-bearded old goat who thinks himself a sprightly young gallant.

PIERS.   If he be old, why does he think himself young?

(PEDLAR *taps his head.*)

(*Understandingly.*) Poor soul, poor soul! Ay, there be many thus. Now my sister's husband's uncle—by marriage—as he grew old he started to think he was a——

PEDLAR.   Let be, let be! There's no time for tales. Listen. He'll come to you to make him clothes. And if you want to line your pockets with silver, you'll listen to him, measure him, take his pay, cut your cloth, and——

PIERS (*propping himself against the table and wailing*). Eh dear, eh dear! Saw ye ever the like? Was there ever a man as unlucky as myself? The first real chance to ply my trade——

PEDLAR.   What ails the man? Is it a pain that's come on ye?

PIERS.   Pain! What pain can there be worse than the chance of earning good money and the means of earning it gone? Why, man, I've broken my needle—and there's not another to be had in the village.

PEDLAR. You've forgotten my new trade. What's a pedlar for but to sell you such things. (*He glances round to make sure* MARTHA *isn't in earshot.*) Now, here's a needle you can have for a penny.

PIERS. Done! Here's your money. Now, lead me to your gentleman.

PEDLAR. No need. He's to come back here. See you humour him. And listen. This fine fellow never tarries long in a place unless some maid is kind to him. Know ye of any in the village can fill his time whilst you make the suit?

PIERS. I've two daughters well worth the time of any man. I'll call them—but their mother had best not know. (PIERS *trots back-stage and calls off left.*) Meg! Lucy! Here, here, I say! (*As he rejoins the* PEDLAR.) A fine pair of maids! Like their dad they've been from the first, the pretty little dears!

PEDLAR. Well, fortune must needs have favoured them if she but keep to custom.

(MEG *and* LUCY *run in.*)

PIERS. Ah, we have a task for you, my daughters.

LUCY. What, Father?

MEG. Oh, Father, you have a needle again.

PIERS. I've just bought it off this pedlar, child.

LUCY. I wish we had our choice of all the fine things in his pack.

PIERS. You are like to have, if you'll but listen.

GILL'S VOICE (*off*). Piers!

PIERS. Coming, sweeting, coming! (*To the girls.*) Listen to the pedlar. He'll tell you all.

GILL (*off*). Piers!

PIERS. Ay, ay, my chuck! I run, I run!

(PIERS *trots out left.*)

MEG.   What is the matter with Father?

PEDLAR.   If you listen I'll tell you how to earn the trinkets you so much wish for.

LUCY.   How is it possible?

MEG.   How can we earn money?

PEDLAR.   I didn't say ye were to earn money. But you can win your gauze and laces if you wish. All there is to do is to humour a gentle madman that will soon be here——

MEG.   A madman!

LUCY.   Oh, this frightens me!

PEDLAR.   He'll not harm you. He's old and grey and his madness takes the strange form of thinking himself young. He loves to talk to young maids, and, if there be the means, he buys them fairings and presents. You need but to flatter him and call him handsome. Forget his whiskers——

MEG.   But——

PEDLAR.   Your father knows of this. You're to keep the gallant here with you whilst your father has started a fine suit for him. Your father gets silver for his suit; you get the ribbons and fineries; I get silver for my goods, and——

(DICKON *has come in and is standing near.*)

DICKON.   And what does Dickon get? Dickon is always forgotten.

(*The* PEDLAR, *after only a second's hesitation, takes* DICKON *aside. The girls are again examining the* PEDLAR's *pack. Whilst the* PEDLAR *and* DICKON *are talking,* GILL *comes in and drags the girls off left.*)

PEDLAR.   Listen.   Would you earn silver too?   Silver of your very own?

DICKON. To spend as I please? To buy trinkets with? Tell me!

PEDLAR. Of all things this quaint madman loves a fowl, ready for the pot. Doubt not he'll pay you well for one.

DICKON. But where am I to get a chicken?

PEDLAR. What ails your finding one in the field behind Gill's house?

DICKON. Nay, that would be stealing!

PEDLAR. Stealing? Did Gill make the hens, then? What right has a woman who bought eggs to call chickens hers? She bought *eggs*, didn't she?

DICKON. Ay, that's true.

PEDLAR. And when shells are cracked and the egg runs out, the egg is lost, isn't it?

DICKON. Ay.

PEDLAR. And those who owned the cracked eggs have nothing?

DICKON (*with a look of delighted inspiration*). A-ay!

PEDLAR. Then when the egg is cracked and the chick which was the egg runs forth, the owner of the egg loses all and the chickens are waste to be picked up by all who will.

DICKON. That sounds fine—but it leaves me amazed.

PEDLAR. Never trouble to be amazed, man. Go and get your chicken quick—quick! For here comes our ancient gallant back again.

(PEDLAR *pushes* DICKON *off left.* MATTHEW *re-enters down-stage left.* LANDLORD *comes out of the inn.*)

LANDLORD. Ah, here's your ale, sir. There and back again all in a minute, as ye might say. Now, if you'd had to wait for Hodge, why, ye might—ye might——

PEDLAR   (*strolling down to take his own ale*). He might have been away, done some business and come back again, eh?

LANDLORD   (*with a chuckle*). Ay, that he might, sir, that he might. He might have been away and done a deal o' business. Well, now I've got to rush off again; no time for gossiping. Tib, you hurry there. And if I'm wanted, come and fetch me. (*He goes back into inn.*)

PEDLAR.   Have you the money?

MATTHEW.   Here it is.

(*He pushes gold across the table.*)

PEDLAR   (*counting and pocketing the money*). Now, are ye ready?

MATTHEW.   But these clothes? They're not the gear of a young man. Had I not better wait, think you, and buy a new suit?

PEDLAR.   It's true ye'll need a new suit, but never wait for that. I'll find ye a tailor. Never fear to go to the girls, though. They'll be too taken up with your face and figure to notice your clothes.

MATTHEW.   Are you going to say the words over me now?

PEDLAR.   You're sure you want me to? You're sure you're ready?

MATTHEW.   Of course I'm ready. Every moment's precious.

PEDLAR.   Very well. (*He picks up a stool and carries it centre.*) Sit perfectly still, here, and close your eyes. Now, cross your fingers, so. (*He makes* MATTHEW *hold one arm aloft with crossed fingers. There is a pause.*) Are you ready?

MATTHEW (*jumping up impatiently*). Curse the man! I believe you're an impostor. Now it's come to the point you can't do it.

PEDLAR (*in an awe-inspiring voice*). Beware how you provoke me. (*He makes a gesture to* MATTHEW, *who sits again.*) Close your eyes, cross your fingers—and wait! (PEDLAR *begins to prowl mysteriously round* MATTHEW, *who sits flinching in increasing terror at each word.*) Hocussy, pocussy—dominus—vimini—militi—grex; instaminis vumini—flummery—jummery—boojah—VIX!

(PEDLAR *gives a piercing whistle, dying down to the sizzle of a rocket.*)

MATTHEW (*opening his eyes and gingerly feeling his arms and legs*). And now, am I—am I—young? (*He rises.*)

PEDLAR (*as he replaces stool*). Faith, it would be harder to find a prettier man in all the country.

MATTHEW (*stretching and posturing*). Yes . . . yes . . . ay—I feel young. My limbs are sprightly. See—see! I can dance. (*He begins to skip about.*) Ow! But that felt plaguily like my gout!

(MEG *and* LUCY *have crept timidly back again.*)

PEDLAR. Oh, I didn't bargain to change your inside. Only your looks. The complete transformation will cost you much more. What, have you never heard of the man who sold his soul for twenty years of youth?

MATTHEW (*crossing himself*). Marry, but that's a hard bargain. Ye'll be asking for my soul next. Here, I don't ——Hadn't you better——

PEDLAR. Nonsense, man! Don't look forward to a thunderstorm. (*With a meaning glance at the girls back-*

stage.) Make hay whilst the sun shines! (*Calling to* MEG *and* LUCY.) Well, my kittens, is there aught there you fancy?

MEG. Oh, Pedlar, such lovely things—had we but the means of buying them.

LUCY (*coming down-stage with a piece of lawn over her shoulder*). Saw ye ever aught softer, finer, or whiter than this?

MATTHEW. Faith, ay, and that's the shoulder that it's lying on! Your shoulder shames the lawn, my dear!

LUCY. Fie, sir, were you old and fatherly, we might think you spoke the truth. But there's no faith to be put in a man so young and handsome, is there, sister?

(MEG *has come down with the* PEDLAR, *who brings his pack with him.*)

MEG. No, indeed. Truly we must not listen.

MATTHEW (*picking out a pair of stockings*). Here's fine things. Come, I'll wager you've already set longing eyes on these. Now, to see these move in and out under a petti-coat at a dance——

MEG. Oh, I dearly love a dance!

MATTHEW. And I, too, my dear. But yesterday I saw— I mean—I was learning a new step—lately come from France. (*He begins tripping and posturing.*) Right foot, left foot. *Pas à droit—pas à gauche—volante* . . . oh, a fine dance!

LUCY (*clapping*). A court dance! A court dance! And with what grace you can turn it!

MEG. Faith, I never saw legs and feet move in such rhythm. (*To* PEDLAR.) Save when the old ram caught his horns in a thicket.

LUCY. Ah, sir, you'd scorn our poor village dances.

MATTHEW. I'd scorn nothing you could teach me. Come!
(*He puts his arms round her.*)

LUCY. Faith, I've still got the pedlar's lawn on my
shoulder.

MATTHEW. No, no. You shall not put it back. Keep
it as a fairing. Hi, Pedlar, here's silver for the lawn on the
maid's shoulders. And here's more silver for the
stockings——

MEG. Oh, no, sir, indeed you must not——

(*But she keeps a firm hand on the stockings.*)

MATTHEW. I'll take no refusal. Besides, the pedlar has
the money now. Come, you shall teach me one of your
dances.

LUCY. But I'm ashamed to dance before one so sprightly
and accomplished.

MEG. And surely we do wrong to talk to one so young.

MATTHEW. No, no! A dance, a dance! Can ye pipe,
Pedlar?

(PEDLAR *produces a pipe. They begin to dance a
sort of hey, the girls pushing and pulling* MATTHEW
*into place; laughing and praising his dancing. As
they work it up we hear, off-stage left, the sounds
of a hen, pursued, caught, and. strangled. When
hen-strangling and dance are at their loudest,*
BARBARA, MATTHEW'S *wife, sweeps in. She is a
large, imposing woman, not unlike the* DUCHESS *in
"Alice". She is dressed in a r'ch, ample gown,
with a towering head-dress. She descends on the
dancers.*)

BARBARA. What, in the name of all the saints in heaven!

MATTHEW. My wife! (*He is taken aback for a second. Then remembers his "transformation" and banks on her not recognizing him. To* PEDLAR.) Play on sir, play on!

BARBARA (*blocking their way*). Play on, indeed! Art mad?

MATTHEW. Out of my way, old woman! You do not know me. I am young enough to be your grandson. Stop not the innocent pleasures of youth.

BARBARA. The man's stark mad. Am I your wife or am I not?

(*There is a burst of laughter from the girls.* BARBARA *turns majestically to inspect them.*)

MATTHEW (*aside to* PEDLAR). You're sure the spell's not wearing off? How old do I look?

PEDLAR. Not a day more than twenty.

BARBARA. And who are these hussies you're gallivanting with?

MEG AND LUCY (*together*). Hussies, indeed? Did you ever hear the like! What right have you to spoil our fun?

MATTHEW. The woman's mad. Do I look as if she were my wife? Does spring mate with winter?

LUCY. Perhaps she's your mother!

MEG. Grandmother, more like!

MATTHEW. You see, gammer? You hear what these my little playmates say—my innocent little playmates! Now, leave us to our frolic. Pipe up, Pedlar. La-di-da-di-dee——

BARBARA. Stark, staring mad! I'll have you in Bedlam before the day's out! Where's the watch? Help! Help!

(*As* BARBARA *runs off right screaming "Help!" her cry is echoed, on the same note, from the left by* GILL.)

GILL (*off-stage left*). Thief! Thief! Out, harrow! Thief! Help!

> (DICKON *dashes on, a fowl in his hand and* GILL *at his heels.*)

GILL (*coming to rest stage centre.* DICKON *is cowering down-stage of his cottage*). So your mother's set you on to do this, you good-for-nothing, has she, since you can do naught else! But I'll teach you, my lad! Ay, and I'll teach her too! Martha! Martha! Out ye come—I'll have ye taken to the justice! Where's the Constable of the watch! Priest's house, indeed! Den o' thieves, more like!

> (*The crowd is gathering. The* PEDLAR *is sitting cross-legged on the table, watching the fun. He is cracking nuts, occasionally flicking one into* TIB's *gaping mouth.*)

MARTHA (*coming out of the cottage*). Is Bedlam let loose, or what is it?

GILL (*as soon as she catches sight of her*). Ye lying, thieving slut! Ye——

MARTHA. Slut, am I? Lying, am I? Thieving, am I? (*She descends threateningly on* GILL.)

GILL. Ye're the mother of the disgrace of the village. If I'd a son turned thief I'd hide my head for shame!

MARTHA. Oh, indeed! And if you watched your own daughters instead of prying on other folks' sons, ye'd be doing better mother's work!

GILL. What's my daughters to do with you? Do they steal chickens?

MARTHA. No! But they're good hands at plucking male birds!

GILL. You say one word against my daughters——

MARTHA.   You dare lay your tongue on my son's good
name——

GILL.   What? When the bird's in his hand!

MARTHA.   Me! The priest's housekeeper!

GILL.   Your son's a thief!

MARTHA.   And if I were to tell you what your daughters
were——

GILL.   Say it again!

MARTHA.   I didn't say it!

GILL.   You called 'em——

MARTHA.   Nay, I didn't. But you seem to know!

GILL.   You dirty slut! You blotch-eyed dodderer! You
skimpy maypole——

MARTHA.   Ye stuffed-out sack-o'-nowt! Ye lying cater-
wauling——

> (*Both women are screaming incoherently and now
> fly at each other.* GILL *gets her teeth into* MARTHA's
> *arm.* MARTHA *does good work with* GILL's *hair.*)

GILL.   Ow—ow!!! Piers! Piers!! If you were a man
you'd defend your wife!

MARTHA.   Ae—eee! Dickon, Dickon! Are ye going to
stand by and see your mother murdered!

> (MEG *and* LUCY *are holding* DICKON. PIERS *runs in
> with a piece of cloth over his arm, needle in hand,
> and circles ineffectively round the scrap.*)

PIERS.   Eh, dear! eh, dear! What's to do now? Oh, my
poor Gill! Help! Help!

> (*The* LANDLORD *has come out. The* PEDLAR *still sits
> on the table.* DICKON *is arguing with* MEG *and*
> LUCY *about the fowl.* MATTHEW *has taken refuge
> round the far side of the inn table.* BARBARA *comes*

back with the CONSTABLE *and one* ASSISTANT. *She ploughs her way through the scrum in the centre of the stage, flinging* MARTHA *and* GILL *to right and left of her.*)

BARBARA.   Are all the lunatics at large now? Where's my husband? Where's he gone?

(GILL *and* MARTHA *re-engage.* BARBARA *sees* MEG *and* LUCY.)

BARBARA.   Ah, there you are, ye brazen hussies! What have you done with my husband?

LUCY. ⎱ Done with your husband?
MEG. ⎰ What should we want with any husband of yours?

(PIERS, *with sudden inspiration, has rescued his wife by jabbing* MARTHA *with the needle.*)

MARTHA.   Aowh!!! (*She turns.*) A needle! My needle! My needle, I'll be bound!

PIERS (*backing away*). Nay, faith. I bought it off the pedlar.

MARTHA.   That's a lie. I asked him for one and he'd none. Ye brazen thief! It's mine ye've got! Mine!

(MARTHA *sets off round the stage in chase of* PIERS. GILL *sees her chance and makes for* DICKON. BARBARA *has just seen* MATTHEW; *she dashes across.*)

PIERS.   Help, help! Gill! It's me she's after now!

(GILL, MARTHA, BARBARA *all secure their prey at the same moment. They drag their victims up centre to* CONSTABLE.)

BARBARA.   Here he is, master Constable. Here's your man!

GILL.   Here's the thief, Constable!

MARTHA.   Here you are, Constable. Here's the thief!

CONSTABLE.   Plague on the women! How can I take 'em all in charge? Has the whole village gone mad?

>   (JAKES, *the* ASSISTANT, *has hold of a man in each*
>   *hand. The* CONSTABLE *has hold of* DICKON.)

We'll have to record their complaints. Out with your pen and parchment, man!

JAKES.   How the devil can I, with my hands full o' thieves? How about fixing 'em in the stocks first?

CONSTABLE.   Nay, there'd be a habeas corpus or some such bother——

>   (*With a howl of misery the* PRIEST *dashes out of his*
>   *cottage, holding his head. He circles blindly round*
>   *the stage.*)

PRIEST.   Oh, the bees! The bees! Holy saints, how they sting! O-oh!

BARBARA.   Another madman!

PRIEST.   O-oh, what's come to them? They've never done this before.

MARTHA.   There's never been a how-de-do like this before.

GILL.   And there's little likelihood of peace whilst thieves run free.

MARTHA.   You've some room to cry thief, when your own husband——

PRIEST.   Oh, Martha, Martha, are you there! Can't you help me? Oh, do something——

>   (MARTHA *goes into cottage with* PRIEST.)

GILL.   You'd think the Devil himself were abroad.

MATTHEW. What's that you're saying? The Devil?
You're right, he *is* here!

CROWD. What's he saying? What's this about the
Devil? (*Etc.*).

BARBARA. Haven't you made fool enough of yourself for
one day?

MATTHEW. I tell you he's here! It's the truth. He
worked a spell on me, and made me young and handsome——

BARBARA. Made you what?

(*There is a roar of laughter from the crowd.*)

Let him go, master Constable, let him go! He's past anything that prison or Bedlam can do for him. He's coming
home with me, and I'll right him.

> (BARBARA *begins to haul* MATTHEW *across to down-
> stage left.*)

MATTHEW. By all that's holy, I tell you the Devil's here!

GILL. Where?

MATTHEW (*pointing to* PEDLAR). There!

> (*Most of crowd shrink over towards* PRIEST's *cottage.
> The* PEDLAR *laughs and pulls faces at them.*)

DICKON. Indeed, it was he bade me take the fowl.
O-oh——it was the Devil tempted me!

MEG AND LUCY (*throwing down their spoils*). And
these are from the Devil's pack!

PIERS. He sold me a needle that nigh cost me my life!

MATTHEW. He sold me back my youth. He tempted me
with talk of girls——

> (BARBARA *waves him to be silent. The* PRIEST *comes
> out again.*)

PRIEST. Friends, friends! What is it now?

CROWD (*turning their back on* PEDLAR *and crowding round* PRIEST). We've caught the Devil! The Devil's here! Defend us from the Devil!

MARTHA. He blinded the eyes of my poor lamb and set him fowl-stealing!

GILL. He sold my Piers a stolen needle!

PIERS. He tempted my poor girls with ribbons.

MATTHEW. He came near asking my soul from me, but with great cunning I bargained for a sample——

PRIEST. Yes, yes, my friends. But—*where is he?*

MATTHEW AND PIERS. Why—he's——

GILL. He's *gone*!

> (*For whilst they have been arguing,* TIB *has slipped from her seat, beckoned to the* PEDLAR, *and led him into the inn.*)

CROWD. He's gone! He's disappeared! (*Etc., etc.*)

CONSTABLE. Why didn't you hold him?

JAKES. Hold him yourself! Why should I handle the Devil?

MATTHEW. Well, so long as he has gone let's all be thankful!

BARBARA. You'll have something to be thankful for when I get you home, my beauty!

LANDLORD (*pointing to the pack which has been left on the table*). Why, yon pedlar's gone and left his pack behind him!

CONSTABLE. Can't you understand? That wasn't no pedlar! It was the Devil!

LANDLORD. You mean—The Devil?

CONSTABLE. Ay, man. The Devil.

LANDLORD. The Devil has sat here and drunk my best ale?

MATTHEW. That he has, landlord—and I paid for it!

LANDLORD. Then I shall put the price up. "As sold to the Devil, on this very spot." E-eh—there isn't another inn i' (Yorkshire) 'at can say that!

GILL. What are you going to do with his pack?

PIERS. Best hand it to the watch.

CONSTABLE. Nay, we're having no truck wi' such goods. He'll happen be coming back for it.

JAKES. I say, give it to the priest. If he does come back he'll be equal to him.

CROWD. Ay, that's it! Give it to the priest! Hand the pack to the priest!

PRIEST. Thank you, friends, thank you, for your—er —confidence in me. I have a plan by which we can prove whether this was indeed the Devil.

CROWD. How? How can we prove it? Oh, don't take any risks!

PRIEST. We will leave the pack here, and you will watch all the roads into the village, and the paths over the fields. If he is the Devil, he will return in spite of your vigilance. If he is merely a trickster you will catch him.

(*He solemnly places the pack in the centre of the stage and stands over it.*)

But, first, my friends, tell me—is there anyone here who would risk taking aught from the Devil's pack?

CROWD. Oh, no! Touch the Devil's pack? No! (*Etc.*)

PRIEST. Good. Now, to your posts. If you catch the pedlar, bring him here.

CROWD. Agreed! Agreed!

(*All hurry out. The pack remains in the centre of
an empty stage. One by one, and cautiously, the
villagers return.* MEG *and* LUCY *come and rescue
the lawn and stockings they threw down.* BARBARA
secures the bag of gold the PEDLAR *had left in his
pack.* GILL *rummages, finds her prize, and then
remembers the chicken. She is about to pick it
up when* DICKON'S *hand and arm comes from the
cottage door and drags it away.* GILL *suppresses
a scream and waddles off.* PIERS *and* MARTHA
*enter from opposite sides; see each other and walk
away, aping innocence. After a few seconds* PIERS
*returns and bears away the whole pack. Another
very short pause.* TIB *peeps out of the inn door,
beckons the* PEDLAR, *who circles the stage in search
of his pack, followed by* TIB *who earnestly imitates
his movements.* TIB *catches sight of the* PRIEST
coming and drags the PEDLAR *into shelter round
the corner of the inn. The* PRIEST *comes out; sees
the empty stage where the pack had been. He
lifts his hands in horror, crosses himself.*)

PRIEST. Friends! Friends!

(*The villagers flock in.*)

Friends, it is proven! The pack has gone! The Devil has
indeed been in our midst!

PEDLAR (*as the curtain falls*). The devil he has!

THE MONKEY'S PAW

A STORY IN THREE SCENES

by

W. W. JACOBS

Dramatized by

LOUIS N. PARKER

CHARACTERS

Mr. White

Mrs. White

Herbert

Sergeant-Major Morris

Mr. Sampson

SCENE: The living-room of an old-fashioned cottage on the outskirts of **Fulham**, London, at the beginning of **the** present century.

THE MONKEY'S PAW

The living-room of an old-fashioned cottage on the out-skirts of Fulham. Set corner-wise in the left angle at the back a deep window; further front, left, three or four steps lead up to a door. Further forward a dresser, with plates, glasses, etc. Right centre, at back, an alcove with the street door fully visible. On the inside of the street door, a wire letter-box. On the right a cupboard, then a fireplace. In the centre a round table. Against the wall, left back, an old-fashioned piano. A comfortable armchair each side of the fireplace. Other chairs. On the mantelpiece a clock, old china figures, etc. An air of comfort pervades the room.

SCENE ONE: *At the rise of the curtain,* MRS. WHITE, *a pleasant-looking old woman, is seated in the armchair below the fire, attending to a kettle which is steaming on the fire, and keeping a laughing eye on* MR. WHITE *and* HERBERT. *These two are seated at the right angle of the table nearest the fire with a chess-board between them.* MR. WHITE *is evidently losing. His hair is ruffled; his spectacles are high up on his forehead.*

HERBERT, *a fine young fellow, is looking with satisfaction at the move he has just made.* MR. WHITE *makes several attempts to move, but thinks better of them. There is a shaded lamp on the table. The door is tightly shut. The curtains of the window are drawn; but every now and then the wind is heard whistling outside.*

MR. WHITE *(moving at last, and triumphant).* There, Herbert, my boy! Got you, I think.

HERBERT. Oh, you're a deep'un, Dad, aren't you?

MRS. WHITE. Mean to say he's beaten you at last?

HERBERT. Lor, no! Why, he's overlooked——

MR. WHITE *(very excited).* I see it! Lemme have that back!

HERBERT. Not much. Rules of the game!

MR. WHITE *(disgusted).* I don't hold with them scientific rules. You turn what ought to be an innocent relaxation——

MRS. WHITE. Don't talk so much, Father. You put him off——

HERBERT *(laughing).* Not he!

MR. WHITE *(trying to distract his attention).* Hark at the wind.

HERBERT *(drily).* Ah! I'm listening. Check.

MR. WHITE *(still trying to distract him).* I should hardly think Sergeant-Major Morris'd come to-night.

HERBERT. Mate. *(Rises and goes up left.)*

MR. WHITE *(with an outbreak of disgust and sweeping the chessmen off the board).* That's the worst of living so far out. Your friends can't come for a quiet chat, and you addle your brains over a confounded——

HERBERT. Now, Father! Morris'll turn up all right.

MR. WHITE (*still in a temper*). Lovers' Lane, Fulham! Ho! of all the beastly, slushy, out-o'-the-way places to live in——! Pathway's a bog, and the road's a torrent. (*To* MRS. WHITE *who has risen, and is at his side.*) What's the County Council thinking of, that's what I want to know? Because this is the only house in the road it doesn't matter if nobody can get near it, I s'pose.

MRS. WHITE. Never mind, dear. Perhaps you'll win to-morrow. (*She moves to back of table.*)

MR. WHITE. Perhaps I'll—perhaps I'll——! What d'you mean? (*Bursts out laughing.*) There! You always know what's going on inside o' me, don't you, Mother?

MRS. WHITE. Ought to, after thirty years, John.

(*She goes to dresser, and busies herself wiping tumblers on tray there.*)

(*He rises, goes to fireplace and lights pipe.*)

HERBERT (*down centre*). And it's not such a bad place, Dad, after all. One of the few old-fashioned houses left near London. None o' your stucco villas. Home-like, I call it. And so do you, or you wouldn't ha' bought it. (*Rolls a cigarette.*)

MR. WHITE (*growling*). Nice job I made o' that, too! With two hundred pounds owin' on it.

HERBERT (*on back of chair, centre*). Why, I shall work that off in no time, Dad. Matter o' three years, with the rise promised me.

MR. WHITE. If you don't get married.

HERBERT. Not me. Not that sort.

MRS. WHITE. I wish you would, Herbert. A good, steady, lad——

(*She brings the tray with a bottle of whisky, glasses, a lemon, spoons, buns, and a knife to the table.*)

HERBERT. Lots o' time, Mother. Sufficient for the day —as the saying goes. Just now my dynamos don't leave me any time for love-making. Jealous they are, I tell you!

MR. WHITE (*chuckling*). I lay awake o' night often, and think: If Herbert took a nap, and let his what-d'you-call-ums—dynamos, run down, all Fulham would be in darkness. Lord! what a joke! (*Gets right centre.*)

HERBERT. Joke! And me with the sack! Pretty idea of a joke you've got, I don't think.

(*Knock at outer door.*)

MRS. WHITE. Hark!

(*Knock repeated, louder.*)

MR. WHITE (*going towards door*). That's him. That's the Sergeant-Major. (*He unlocks door, back.*)

HERBERT (*removes chess-board*). Wonder what yarn he's got for us to-night. (*Places chess-board on piano, goes up right, busies himself putting the other armchair nearer fire, etc.*)

MRS. WHITE. Don't let the door slam, John!

> (MR. WHITE *opens door a little, struggling with it. Wind.* SERGEANT-MAJOR MORRIS, *a veteran with a distinct military appearance—left arm gone— dressed as a commissionaire, is seen to enter.* MR. WHITE *helps him off with his coat, which he hangs up in the outer hall.*)

MR. WHITE (*at the door*). Slip in quick! It's as much as I can do to hold it against the wind.

SERGEANT. Awful! Awful! (*Busy taking off his cloak.*)

And a mile up the road—by the cemetery—it's worse. Enough to blow the hair off your head.

MR. WHITE.   Give me your stick.

SERGEANT.   If 'twasn't I knew what a welcome I'd get——

MR. WHITE   (*preceding him into the room*).   Sergeant-Major Morris!

MRS. WHITE.   Tut! tut! So cold you must be! Come to the fire; do'ee, now.

SERGEANT.   How are you, marm? (*To* HERBERT) How's yourself, laddie? Not on duty yet, eh? Day week, eh?

HERBERT   (*centre*).   No, sir. Night week. But there's half an hour yet.

SERGEANT   (*sitting in the armchair above the fire, which* MRS. WHITE *is motioning him towards*).

(MR. WHITE *mixes grog for* MORRIS.)

Thank'ee kindly, marm. That's good—hah! That's a sight better than the trenches at Chitral. That's better than settin' in a puddle with the rain pourin' down in buckets, and the natives takin' pot-shots at you.

MRS. WHITE.   Didn't you have no umbrellas?

(*Corner below fire, kneels before it, stirs it, etc.*)

SERGEANT.   Umbrell——? Ho! ho! That's good! Eh, White? That's good. Did ye hear what she said? Umbrellas! —*And* galoshes! *and* hot-water bottles!—Ho, yes! No offence, marm, but it's easy to see you was never a soldier.

HERBERT   (*rather hurt*).   Mother spoke out o' kindness, sir.

SERGEANT.   And well I know it; and no offence intended. No, marm, 'ardship, 'ardship is the soldier's lot. Starvation, fever, and get yourself shot. That's a bit o' my own.

MRS. WHITE. You don't look to've taken much harm
—except——(*Indicates his empty sleeve. She takes kettle
to table, then returns to fire.*)

SERGEANT (*showing a medal hidden under his coat*).
And that I got this for. No, marm. Tough. Thomas Morris
is tough.

> (MR. WHITE *is holding a glass of grog under the*
> SERGEANT'*s nose.*)

And sober. What's this now?

MR. WHITE. Put your nose in it; you'll see.

SERGEANT. Whisky? And hot? And sugar? And a slice
o' lemon? No. I said I'd never—but seein' the sort o' night.
Well! (*Waving the glass at them.*) Here's another thousand
a year!

MR. WHITE (*sits at table with a glass*). Same to you,
and many of 'em.

SERGEANT (*to* HERBERT, *who has no glass*). What? Not
you?

HERBERT (*laughing and sitting across chair right*). Oh!
'tisn't for want of being sociable. But my work don't go
with it. Not if 'twas ever so little. I've got to keep a cool
head, a steady eye, and a still hand. The fly-wheel might
gobble me up.

MRS. WHITE. Don't, Herbert. (*Sits in armchair below
fire.*)

HERBERT (*laughing*). No fear, Mother.

SERGEANT. Ah! you electricians!—Sort o' magicians, you
are. Light! says you—and light it is. And, power! says you
—and the trams go whizzin'. And knowledge! says you—
and words go 'ummin' to the ends o' the world. It fair beats
me—and I've seen a bit in my time, too.

HERBERT (*nudges his father*). Your Indian magic? All a fake, governor. The fakir's fake.

SERGEANT. Fake, you call it? I tell you, I've seen it.

HERBERT (*nudging his father with his foot*). Oh, come, now! such as what? Come, now!

SERGEANT. I've seen a cove with no more clothes on than a babby, (*to* MRS. WHITE) if you know what I mean—take an empty basket—empty, mind!—as empty as—as this here glass——

MR. WHITE. Hand it over, Morris. (*Hands it to* HERBERT, *who goes quickly behind table and fills it.*)

SERGEANT. Which was not my intentions, but used for illustration.

HERBERT (*while mixing*). Oh, *I've* seen the basket trick; and I've read how it was done. Why, I could do it myself, with a bit o' practice. Ladle out something stronger.

(HERBERT *brings him the glass.*)

SERGEANT. Stronger?—what do you say to an old fakir chuckin' a rope up in the air—in the *air*, mind you!—and swarming up it, same as if it was 'ooked on—and vanishing clean out o' sight?—I've seen *that*.

(HERBERT *goes to table, plunges a knife into a bun and offers it to the* SERGEANT *with exaggerated politeness.*)

SERGEANT (*eyeing it with disgust*). Bun—? What for?

HERBERT. That yarn takes it.

(MR. *and* MRS. WHITE *delighted.*)

SERGEANT. Mean to say you doubt my word?

MRS. WHITE. No, no! He's only taking you off—You shouldn't, Herbert.

MR. WHITE. Herbert always was one for a bit o' fun!

(HERBERT *puts bun back on table, comes round in front, and moving the chair out of the way, sits cross-legged on the floor at his father's side.*)

SERGEANT.   But it's true. Why, if I chose, I could tell you things—But there! you don't get no more yarns out o' *me*.

MR. WHITE.   Nonsense, old friend. (*Puts down his glass.*) You're not going to get shirty about a bit o' fun. (*Moves his chair nearer* MORRIS'S.) What was that you started telling me the other day about a monkey's paw, or something? (*Nudges* HERBERT, *and winks at* MRS. WHITE.)

SERGEANT   (*gravely*). Nothing. Leastways, nothing worth hearing.

MRS. WHITE   (*with astonished curiosity*).   Monkey's paw——?

MR. WHITE.   Ah—you was tellin' me——

SERGEANT.   Nothing. Don't go on about it. (*Puts his empty glass to his lips—then stares at it.*) *What*? Empty again? There! When I begin thinkin' o' the paw, it makes me that absent-minded——

MR. WHITE   (*rises and fills glass*). You said you always carried it on you.

SERGEANT.   So I do, for fear o' what might happen. (*Sunk in thought.*) Ay!—ay!

MR. WHITE   (*handing him his glass refilled*). There.

(*Sits again in same chair.*)

MRS. WHITE.   What's it for?

SERGEANT.   You wouldn't believe me, if I was to tell you.

HERBERT.   *I* will, every word.

SERGEANT.   Magic, then!—Don't you laugh!

HERBERT.   I'm not. Got it on you now?

SERGEANT. Of course.

HERBERT. Let's see it.

(*Seeing the* SERGEANT *embarrassed with his glass,* MRS. WHITE *rises, takes it from him, places it on mantelpiece and remains standing.*)

SERGEANT. Oh, it's nothing to look at. (*Hunting in his pocket.*) Just an ordinary—little paw—dried to a mummy. (*Produces it and holds it towards* MRS. WHITE.) Here.

MRS. WHITE (*who has leant forward eagerly to see it, starts back with a little cry of disgust*). Oh!

HERBERT. Give us a look. (MORRIS *passes the paw to* MR. WHITE, *from whom* HERBERT *takes it.*) Why, it's all dried up!

SERGEANT. I said so.

(*Wind.*)

MRS. WHITE (*with a slight shudder*). Hark at the wind! (*Sits again in her old place.*)

MR. WHITE (*taking the paw from* HERBERT). And what might there be special about it?

SERGEANT (*impressively*). That there paw has had a spell put upon it!

MR. WHITE. No? (*In great alarm he thrusts the paw back into* MORRIS's *hand.*)

SERGEANT (*pensively, holding the paw in the palm of his hand*). Ah! By an old fakir. He was a very holy man. He'd sat all doubled up in one spot, goin' on for fifteen year; thinkin' o' things. And he wanted to show that fate ruled people. That everything was cut and dried from the beginning, as you might say. That there warn't no gettin' away from it. And that, if you tried to, you caught it hot. (*Pauses solemnly.*) So he put a spell on this bit of a paw. It might ha' been anything else, but he took the first thing that came handy. Ah! He put a spell on it, and made it so that three people (*looking at them and with deep meaning*) could each have three wishes.

(*All but* MRS. WHITE *laugh rather nervously.*)

MRS. WHITE. Ssh! Don't!

SERGEANT (*more gravely*). But——! But, mark you, though the wishes was granted, those three people would have cause to wish they *hadn't* been.

MR. WHITE. But how *could* the wishes be granted?

SERGEANT. He didn't say. It would all happen so natural, you might think it a coincidence if so disposed.

HERBERT. Why haven't you tried it, sir?

SERGEANT (*gravely, after a pause*). I have.

HERBERT (*eagerly*). You've had your three wishes?

SERGEANT (*gravely*). Yes.

MRS. WHITE. Were they granted?

SERGEANT (*staring at the fire*). They were.

(*A pause.*)

MR. WHITE. Has anybody else wished?

SERGEANT. Yes. The first owner had his three wish—— (*Lost in recollection.*) Yes, oh yes, he had his three wishes all right. I don't know what his first two were (*very impressively*) but the third was for death. (*All shudder.*) That's how I got the paw.

(*A pause.*)

HERBERT (*cheerfully*). Well! Seems to me you've only got to wish for things that *can't* have any bad luck about 'em—— (*Rises.*)

SERGEANT (*shaking his head*). Ah!

MR. WHITE (*tentatively*). Morris—if you've had your three wishes—it's no good to you, now—what do you keep it for?

SERGEANT (*still holding the paw; looking at it*). Fancy, I s'pose. I did have some idea of selling it, but I don't think I will. It's done mischief enough already. Besides, people won't buy. Some of 'em think it's a fairy tale. And some want to try it first, and pay after.

(*Nervous laugh from the others.*)

MRS. WHITE. If you could have another three wishes, would you?

SERGEANT (*slowly—weighing the paw in his hand, and looking at it*). I don't know—I don't know—(*Suddenly, with violence, flinging it in the fire.*) No! I'm damned if I would!

(*Movement from all.*)

MR. WHITE (*rises and quickly snatches it out of the fire*). What are you doing?

(WHITE *goes right centre.*)

SERGEANT (*rising and following him and trying to prevent him*). Let it burn! Let the infernal thing burn!

MRS. WHITE (*rises*). Let it burn, Father!

MR. WHITE (*wiping it on his coat-sleeve*). No. If you don't want it, give it to me.

SERGEANT. I won't! I won't! My hands are clear of it. I threw it on the fire. If you keep it, don't blame me, whatever happens. Here! Pitch it back again.

MR. WHITE (*stubbornly*). I'm going to keep it. What do you say, Herbert?

HERBERT (*left centre, laughing*). I say, keep it if you want to. Stuff and nonsense, anyhow.

MR. WHITE (*looking at the paw thoughtfully*). Stuff and nonsense. Yes. I wonder—(*casually*) I wish—— (*He was going to say some ordinary thing, like "I wish I were certain."*)

SERGEANT (*misunderstanding him; violently*). Stop! Mind what you're doing. That's not the way.

MR. WHITE. What *is* the way?

MRS. WHITE (*moving away up right centre to back of table and beginning to put the tumblers straight, and the chairs in their places*). Oh, don't have anything to do with it, John.

> (*Takes glasses on tray to dresser, and busies herself there, rinsing them in a bowl of water on the dresser, and wiping them with a cloth.*)

SERGEANT. That's what I say, marm. But if I warn't to tell him, he might go wishing something he didn't mean to. You hold it in your right hand, and wish aloud. But I warn you! I warn you!

MRS. WHITE. Sounds like the *Arabian Nights*. Don't you think you might wish me four pair o' hands?

MR. WHITE (*laughing*). Right you are, Mother!—I wish——

SERGEANT (*pulling his arm down*). Stop it! If you must wish, wish for something sensible. Look here! I can't stand this. Gets on my nerves. Where's my coat? (*Goes into alcove.*)

> (*MR. WHITE crosses to fireplace and carefully puts the paw on mantelpiece. He is absorbed in it to the end of the tableau.*)

HERBERT. I'm coming your way, to the works, in a

minute. Won't you wait? (*Goes up centre, helps* MORRIS *with his coat.*)

SERGEANT (*putting on his coat*). No. I'm all shook up. I want fresh air. I don't want to be here when you wish. And wish you will as soon's my back's turned. I know. I know. But I've warned you, mind.

MR. WHITE (*helping him into his coat*). All right, Morris. Don't you fret about us. (*Gives him money.*) Here.

SERGEANT (*refusing it*). No, I won't——

MR. WHITE (*forcing it into his hand*). Yes, you will. (*Opens door.*)

SERGEANT (*turning to the room*). Well, good-night all. (*To* WHITE.) Put it in the fire.

ALL. Good-night.

> (*Exit* SERGEANT. MR. WHITE *closes door, comes to-wards fireplace, absorbed in the paw.*)

HERBERT (*down left*). If there's no more in this than there is in his other stories, we shan't make much out of it.

MRS. WHITE (*comes down right centre to* WHITE). Did you give him anything for it, Father?

MR. WHITE. A trifle. He didn't want it, but I made him take it.

MRS. WHITE. There, now! You shouldn't. Throwing your money about.

MR. WHITE (*looking at the paw which he has picked up again*). I wonder——

HERBERT. What?

MR. WHITE. I wonder, whether we hadn't better chuck it on the fire?

HERBERT (*laughing*). Likely! Why, we're all going to be rich and famous, and happy.

MRS. WHITE. Throw it on the fire, indeed, when you've given money for it! So like you, Father.

HERBERT. Wish to be an Emperor, Father, to begin with. Then you can't be henpecked!

MRS. WHITE (*going for him front of table with a duster*). You young——! (*Follows him to back of table.*)

HERBERT (*running away from her round behind table*). Steady with that duster, Mother!

MR. WHITE. Be quiet, there! (HERBERT *catches* MRS. WHITE *in his arms and kisses her.*) I wonder——(*He has the paw in his hand.*) I don't know what to wish for, and that's a fact. (*He looks about him with a happy smile.*) I seem to've got all I want.

HERBERT (*with his hands on the old man's shoulders*). Old Dad! If you'd only cleared the debt on the house, you'd be quite happy, wouldn't you? (*Laughing.*) Well—go ahead!—wish for the two hundred pounds: that'll just do it.

MR. WHITE (*half laughing*). Shall I?

(*Crosses to right centre.*)

HERBERT. Go on! Here!—I'll play slow music.

(*Crosses to piano.*)

MRS. WHITE. Don't 'ee, John. Don't have nothing to do with it!

HERBERT. Now, Dad. (*Plays.*)

MR. WHITE. I will! (*Holds up the paw, as if half ashamed.*) I wish for two hundred pounds.

(*Crash on the piano. At the same instant* MR. WHITE *utters a cry and lets the paw drop.*)

MRS. WHITE and HERBERT. } What's the matter?

MR. WHITE (*gazing with horror at the paw*). It moved! As I wished, it twisted in my hand like a snake.

HERBERT (*goes down right and picks the paw up*). Nonsense, Dad. Why, it's as stiff as a bone. (*Lays it on the mantelpiece.*)

MRS. WHITE. Must have been your fancy, Father.

HERBERT (*laughing*). Well——? (*Looking round the room.*) I don't see the money; and I bet I never shall.

MR. WHITE (*relieved*). Thank God, there's no harm done! But it gave me a shock.

HERBERT. Half-past eleven. I must get along. I'm on at midnight. (*Goes up centre, fetches his coat, etc.*) We've had quite a merry evening.

MRS. WHITE. I'm off to bed. Don't be late for breakfast, Herbert.

HERBERT. I shall walk home as usual. Does me good. I shall be with you about nine. Don't wait, though.

MRS. WHITE. You know your father never waits.

HERBERT. Good-night, Mother. (*Kisses her. She lights candle on dresser, left, goes up stairs and exit.*) HERBERT (*coming to his father, left, who is sunk in thought*). Good-night, Dad. You'll find the cash tied up in the middle of the bed.

MR. WHITE (*staring, seizes HERBERT's hand*). It moved, Herbert.

HERBERT. Ah! And a monkey hanging by his tail from the bed-post, watching you count the golden sovereigns.

MR. WHITE (*accompanying him to the door*). I wish you wouldn't joke, my boy.

HERBERT. All right, Dad. (*Opens door.*) Lord! What weather! Good-night. (*Exit.*)

(*The old man shakes his head, closes the door, locks it, puts the chain up, slips the lower bolt, has some difficulty with the upper bolt.*)

MR. WHITE. This bolt's stiff again! I must get Herbert to look to it in the morning.

(*Comes into the room, puts out the lamp, crosses towards steps; but is irresistibly attracted towards fireplace. Sits down and stares into the fire. His expression changes: he sees something horrible.*)

MR. WHITE (*with an involuntary cry*). Mother! Mother!

MRS. WHITE (*appearing at the door at the top of the steps with candle*). What's the matter? (*Comes down right centre.*)

MR. WHITE (*mastering himself. Rises*). Nothing—I— haha!—I saw faces in the fire.

MRS. WHITE. Come along.

(*She takes his arm and draws him towards the steps. He looks back, frightened, towards fireplace as they reach the first step.*)

TABLEAU CURTAIN

SCENE TWO: *Bright sunshine. The table, which has been moved nearer the window, is laid for breakfast.* MRS. WHITE *busy about the table.* MR. WHITE *standing in the window looking off right. The inner door is open, showing the outer door.*

MR. WHITE. What a morning Herbert's got for walking home!

MRS. WHITE (*left centre*). What's o'clock? (*Looks at clock on mantelpiece.*) Quarter to nine, I declare. He's off at eight. (*Crosses to fire.*)

MR. WHITE. Takes him half-an-hour to change and wash. He's just by the cemetery now.

MRS. WHITE. He'll be here in ten minutes.

MR. WHITE (*coming to the table*). What's for breakfast?

MRS. WHITE. Sausages. (*At the mantelpiece.*) Why, if here isn't that dirty monkey's paw! (*Picks it up, looks at it with disgust, puts it back. Takes sausages in dish from before fire and places them on table.*) Silly thing! The idea of us listening to such nonsense!

MR. WHITE (*goes up to window again*). Ay—the Sergeant-Major and his yarns! I suppose all old soldiers are alike——

MRS. WHITE. Come on, Father. Herbert hates us to wait.

(*They both sit and begin breakfast.*)

MRS. WHITE. How could wishes be granted, nowadays?

MR. WHITE. Ah! Been thinking about it all night, have you?

MRS. WHITE. You kept me awake, with your tossing and tumbling——

MR. WHITE. Ay, I had a bad night.

MRS. WHITE. It was the storm, I expect. How it blew!

MR. WHITE. I didn't hear it. I was asleep and not asleep, if you know what I mean.

MRS. WHITE. And all that rubbish about its making you unhappy if your wish was granted! How could two hundred pounds hurt you, eh, Father?

MR. WHITE. Might drop on my head in a lump. Don't see any other way. And I'd try to bear that. Though, mind

THE MONKEY'S PAW

you, Morris said it would all happen so naturally that you might take it for a coincidence, if so disposed.

MRS. WHITE. Well—it hasn't happened. That's all I know. And it isn't going to. (*A letter is seen to drop in the letter-box.*) And how you can sit there and talk about it—— (*Sharp postman's knock; she jumps to her feet.*) What's that?

MR. WHITE. Postman, o' course.

MRS. WHITE (*seeing the letter from a distance; in an awed whisper*). He's brought a letter, John!

MR. WHITE (*laughing*). What did you think he'd bring? Ton o' coals?

MRS. WHITE. John—! John—! Suppose——?

MR. WHITE. Suppose what?

MRS. WHITE. Suppose it was two hundred pounds!

MR. WHITE (*suppressing his excitement*). Eh!—— Here! Don't talk nonsense. Why don't you fetch it?

MRS. WHITE (*crosses and takes letter out of the box*). It's thick, John—(*feels it*)—and—and it's got something crisp inside it. (*Takes letter to* WHITE *right centre.*)

MR. WHITE. Who—who's it for?

MRS. WHITE. You.

MR. WHITE. Hand it over, then. (*Feeling and examining it with ill-concealed excitement.*) The idea! What a superstitious old woman you are! Where are my specs?

MRS. WHITE. Let me open it.

MR. WHITE. Don't you touch it. Where are my specs? (*Goes to right.*)

MRS. WHITE. Don't let sudden wealth sour your temper, John.

MR. WHITE. Will you find my specs?

MRS. WHITE (*taking them off mantelpiece*). Here, John, here.

(*As he opens the letter.*)

Take care! Don't tear it!

MR. WHITE. Tear what?

MRS. WHITE. If it was banknotes, John!

MR. WHITE (*taking a thick, formal document out of the envelope and a crisp-looking slip*). You've gone dotty.— You've made me nervous. (*Reads.*) "Sir,—Enclosed please find receipt for interest on the mortgage of £200 on your house, duly received."

(*They look at each other.* MR. WHITE *sits down to finish his breakfast silently.* MRS. WHITE *goes to the window.*)

MRS. WHITE. That comes of listening to tipsy old soldiers.

MR. WHITE (*pettish*). What does?

MRS. WHITE. You thought there was banknotes in it.

MR. WHITE (*injured*). I didn't! I said all along——

MRS. WHITE. How Herbert will laugh, when I tell him!

MR. WHITE (*with gruff good humour*). You're not going to tell him. You're going to keep your mouth shut. That's what you're going to do. Why, I should never hear the last of it.

MRS. WHITE. Serve you right. I shall tell him. You know you like his fun. See how he joked you last night when you said the paw moved.

(*She is looking through the window towards right.*)

MR. WHITE. So it did. It did move. That I'll swear to.

MRS. WHITE (*abstractedly: she is watching something outside*). You thought it did.

MR. WHITE. I say it did. There was no thinking about it. You saw how it upset me, didn't you?

(*She doesn't answer.*)

Didn't you?—Why don't you listen? (*Turns round.*) What is it?

MRS. WHITE. Nothing.

MR. WHITE (*turns back to his breakfast*). Do you see Herbert coming?

MRS. WHITE. No.

MR. WHITE. He's about due. What is it?

MRS. WHITE. Nothing. Only a man. Looks like a gentleman. Leastways, he's in black, and he's got a top-hat on.

MR. WHITE. What about him? (*He is not interested; goes on eating.*)

MRS. WHITE. He stood at the garden-gate as if he wanted to come in. But he couldn't seem to make up his mind.

MR. WHITE. Oh, go on! You're full o' fancies.

MRS. WHITE. He's going—no; he's coming back.

MR. WHITE. Don't let him see you peeping.

MRS. WHITE (*with increasing excitement*). He's looking at the house. He's got his hand on the latch. No. He turns away again. (*Eagerly.*) John! He looks like a sort of a lawyer.

MR. WHITE. What of it?

MRS. WHITE. Oh, you'll only laugh again. But suppose —suppose he's coming about the two hundred——

MR. WHITE. You're not to mention it again!—You're a foolish old woman.—Come and eat your breakfast. (*Eagerly.*) Where is he now?

MRS. WHITE. Gone down the road. He has turned back.

He seems to've made up his mind. Here he comes!—Oh, John, and me all untidy! (*Crosses to fire R.*)

 (*Knock.*)

MR. WHITE (*to* MRS. WHITE *who is hastily smoothing her hair, etc.*). What's it matter? He's made a mistake. Come to the wrong house. (*Crosses to fireplace.*)

  (MRS. WHITE *opens the door.* MR. SAMPSON, *dressed from head to foot in solemn black, with a top-hat, stands in the doorway.*)

SAMPSON (*outside*). Is this Mr. White's?

MRS. WHITE. Come in, sir. Please step in.

  (*She shows him into the room; he is awkward and nervous.*)

You must overlook our being so untidy; and the room all anyhow; and John in his garden-coat. (*To* MR. WHITE, *reproachfully.*) Oh, John.

SAMPSON (*to* MR. WHITE). Morning. My name is Sampson.

MRS. WHITE (*offering a chair*). Won't you please be seated?

  (SAMPSON *stands quite still up centre.*)

SAMPSON. Ah—thank you—no, I think not—I think not. (*Pause.*)

MR. WHITE (*awkwardly, trying to help him*). Fine weather for the time o' year.

SAMPSON. Ah—yes—yes——(*Pause; he makes a renewed effort.*) My name is Sampson—I've come——

MRS. WHITE. Perhaps you was wishful to see Herbert; he'll be home in a minute. (*Pointing.*) Here's his breakfast waiting——

SAMPSON (*interrupting her hastily*). No, no! (*Pause.*)
I've come from the electrical works——

MRS. WHITE. Why, you might have come *with* him.

> (MR. WHITE *sees something is wrong, tenderly puts
> his hand on her arm.*)

SAMPSON. No—no—I've come—*alone.*

MRS. WHITE (*with a little anxiety*). Is anything the
matter?

SAMPSON. I was asked to call——

MRS. WHITE (*abruptly*). Herbert! Has anything happened? Is he hurt? Is he hurt?

MR. WHITE (*soothing her*). There, there, Mother.
Don't jump to conclusions. Let the gentleman speak. You've
not brought bad news, I'm sure, sir.

SAMPSON. I'm sorry——

MRS. WHITE. Is he hurt?

> (SAMPSON *bows.*)

MRS. WHITE. Badly?

SAMPSON. Very badly. (*Turns away.*)

MRS. WHITE (*with a cry*). John—! (*She instinctively
moves towards* WHITE.)

MR. WHITE. Is he in pain?

SAMPSON. He is not in pain.

MRS. WHITE. Oh, thank God! Thank God for that!
Thank——(*She looks in a startled fashion at* MR. WHITE—
realizes what SAMPSON *means, catches his arm and tries to
turn him towards her.*) Do you mean——?

> (SAMPSON *avoids her look; she gropes for her hus-
> band: he takes her two hands in his and gently
> lets her sink into the armchair above the fireplace,
> then he stands on her right, between her and*
> SAMPSON.)

MR. WHITE   (*hoarsely*). Go on, sir.

SAMPSON.   He was telling his mates a story. Something that had happened here last night. He was laughing, and wasn't noticing and—and—(*hushed*) the machinery caught him——

> (*A little cry from* MRS. WHITE, *her face shows her horror and agony.*)

MR. WHITE   (*vague, holding* MRS. WHITE'*s hand*). The machinery caught him—yes—and him the only child—it's hard, sir—very hard——

SAMPSON   (*subdued*). The Company wished me to convey their sincere sympathy with you in your great loss——

MR. WHITE   (*staring blankly*). Our—great—loss——!

SAMPSON.   I was to say further—(*as if apologizing*) I am only their servant—I am only obeying orders——

MR. WHITE.   Our—great—loss——

SAMPSON   (*laying an envelope on the table and edging towards the door*). I was to say, the Company disclaim all responsibility, but, in consideration of your son's services, they wish to present you with a certain sum as compensation.

> (*Gets to door.*)

MR. WHITE.   Our—great—loss——(*Suddenly, with horror.*) How—how much?

SAMPSON   (*in the doorway*). Two hundred pounds.

> (*Exit.*)

> (MRS. WHITE *gives a cry. The old man takes no heed of her, smiles faintly, puts out his hands like a sightless man, and drops, a senseless heap, to the floor.* MRS. WHITE *stares at him blankly and her hands go out helplessly towards him.*)

TABLEAU CURTAIN

SCENE THREE: *Night. On the table a candle is flickering at its last gasp. The room looks neglected.* MR. WHITE *is dozing fitfully in the armchair.* MRS. WHITE *is in the window peering through the blind towards left.*

(MR. WHITE *starts, wakes, looks around him.*)

MR. WHITE (*fretfully*). Jenny—Jenny.

MRS. WHITE (*in the window*). Yes.

MR. WHITE. Where are you?

MRS. WHITE. At the window.

MR. WHITE. What are you doing?

MRS. WHITE. Looking up the road.

MR. WHITE (*falling back*). What's the use, Jenny? What's the use?

MRS. WHITE. That's where the cemetery is; that's where we've laid him.

MR. WHITE. Ay—ay—a week today—what o'clock is it?

MRS. WHITE. I don't know.

MR. WHITE. We don't take much account of time now, Jenny, do we?

MRS. WHITE. Why should we? He don't come home. He'll never come home again. There's nothing to think about——

MR. WHITE. Or to talk about. (*Pause.*) Come away from the window; you'll get cold.

MRS. WHITE. It's colder where *he* is.

MR. WHITE. Ay—gone for ever——

MRS. WHITE. And taken all our hopes with him——

MR. WHITE. And all our *wishes*——

MRS. WHITE. Ay, and all our— (*With a sudden cry.*) John!

(*She comes quickly to him; he rises.*)

MR. WHITE. Jenny! For God's sake! What's the matter?

MRS. WHITE   (*with dreadful eagerness*). The *paw*! The monkey's paw!

MR. WHITE   (*bewildered*). Where? Where is it? What's wrong with it?

MRS. WHITE.   I want it! You haven't done away with it?

MR. WHITE.   I haven't seen it—since—why?

MRS. WHITE.   I want it! Find it! Find it!

MR. WHITE   (*groping on the mantelpiece*). Here! Here it is! What do you want of it? (*He leaves it there.*)

MRS. WHITE.   Why didn't I think of it? Why didn't you think of it?

MR. WHITE.   Think of what?

MRS. WHITE.   The *other two* wishes!

MR. WHITE   (*with horror*). What?

MRS. WHITE.   We've only had one.

MR. WHITE   (*tragically*). Wasn't that enough?

MRS. WHITE.   No! We'll have one more. (WHITE *crosses to right centre.* MRS. WHITE *takes the paw, and follows him.*) Take it. Take it quickly. And wish——

MR. WHITE   (*avoiding the paw*). Wish what?

MRS. WHITE.   Oh, John! John! Wish our boy alive again!

MR. WHITE.   Good God! Are you mad?

MRS. WHITE.   Take it. Take it and wish. (*With a paroxysm of grief.*) Oh, my boy! My boy!

MR. WHITE.   Get to bed. Get to sleep. You don't know what you're saying.

MRS. WHITE.   We had the first wish granted—why not the second?

MR. WHITE   (*hushed*). He's been dead ten days, and— Jenny! Jenny! I only knew him by his clothing--if you wasn't allowed to see him then—how could you bear to see him *now*?

MRS. WHITE. I don't care. Bring him back.

MR. WHITE (*shrinking from the paw*). I daren't touch it!

MRS. WHITE (*thrusting it in his hand*). Here! Here! Wish!

MR. WHITE (*trembling*). Jenny!

MRS. WHITE (*fiercely*). Wish! (*She goes on frantically whispering "Wish".*)

MR. WHITE (*shuddering, but overcome by her insistence*). I—I—wish—my—son—alive again.

> (*He drops it with a cry. The candle goes out. Utter darkness. He sinks into a chair. MRS. WHITE hurries to the window and draws the blind back. She stands in the moonlight. Pause.*)

MRS. WHITE (*drearily*). Nothing.

MR. WHITE. Thank God! Thank God!

MRS. WHITE. Nothing at all. Along the whole length of the road not a living thing. (*Closes blind.*) And nothing, nothing, nothing left in our lives, John.

MR. WHITE. Except each other, Jenny—and memories.

MRS. WHITE (*coming back slowly to the fireplace*). We're too old. We were only alive in him. We can't begin again. We can't feel anything now, John, but emptiness and darkness. (*She sinks into armchair.*)

MR. WHITE. 'Tisn't for long, Jenny. There's that to look forward to.

MRS. WHITE. Every minute's long, now.

MR. WHITE (*rising*). I can't bear the darkness!

MRS. WHITE. It's dreary—dreary.

MR. WHITE (*crosses to dresser*). Where's the candle? (*Finds it and brings it to table.*) And the matches? Where are the matches? We mustn't sit in the dark. 'Tisn't whole-some. (*Lights match; the other candlestick is close to him.*) There. (*Turning with the lighted match towards* MRS. WHITE, *who is rocking and moaning.*) Don't take on so, Mother.

MRS. WHITE. I'm a mother no longer.

MR. WHITE (*lights candle*). There now; there now. Go on up to bed. Go on, now—I'm a-coming.

MRS. WHITE. Whether I'm here or in bed, or wherever I am, I'm with my boy, I'm with——

  (*A low single knock at the street door.*)

MRS. WHITE (*starting*). What's that!

MR. WHITE (*mastering his horror*). A rat. The house is full of 'em.

  (*A louder single knock; she starts up. He catches her by the arm.*)

Stop! What are you going to do?

MRS. WHITE (*wildly*). It's my boy! It's Herbert! I forgot it was a mile away! What are you holding me for? I must open the door!

  (*The knocking continues in single knocks at irregular intervals, constantly growing louder and more insistent.*)

MR. WHITE (*still holding her*). For God's sake!

MRS. WHITE (*struggling*). Let me go!

MR. WHITE. Don't open the door!

  (*He drags her towards left front.*)

MRS. WHITE. Let me go!

MR. WHITE. Think what you might see!

MRS. WHITE (*struggling fiercely*). Do you think I fear the child I bore! Let me go! (*She wrenches herself loose and rushes to the door which she tears open.*) I'm coming, Herbert! I'm coming!

MR. WHITE   (*cowering in the extreme corner, left front*). Don't 'ee do it! Don't 'ee do it!

> (MRS. WHITE *is at work on the outer door, where the knocking still continues. She slips the chain, slips the lower bolt, unlocks the door.*)

MR. WHITE   (*suddenly*). The paw! Where's the monkey's paw?

> (*He gets on his knees and feels along the floor for it.*)

MRS. WHITE   (*tugging at the top bolt*). John! The top bolt's stuck. I can't move it. Come and help. Quick!

MR. WHITE   (*wildly groping*). The paw! There's a wish left.

> (*The knocking is now loud, and in groups of increasing length between the speeches.*)

MRS. WHITE.   D'ye hear him? John! Your child's knocking!

MR. WHITE.   Where is it? Where did it fall?

MRS. WHITE   (*tugging desperately at the bolt*). Help! Help! Will you keep your child from his home?

MR. WHITE.   Where did it fall? I can't find it—I can't find——

> (*The knocking is now tempestuous and there are blows upon the door as of a body beating against it.*)

MRS. WHITE.   Herbert! Herbert! My boy! Wait! Your mother's opening to you! Ah! It's moving! It's moving!

MR. WHITE.   God forbid! (*Finds the paw.*) Ah!

MRS. WHITE   (*slipping the bolt*). Herbert!

MR. WHITE   (*has raised himself to his knees; he holds the paw high*).   I wish him dead.   (*The knocking stops abruptly.*)   I wish him dead and at peace!

MRS. WHITE   (*flinging the door open simultaneously*).
Herb——

>   (*A flood of moonlight. Emptiness. The old man sways in prayer on his knees. The old woman lies half swooning, wailing against the door-post.*)

CURTAIN

A BATTLE OF WITS

by

NORMAN WILLIAMS

CHARACTERS

Chung Tai

Madam Chung

Silver Lotus

Sun Chu

A Worker

A Property Man

An Attendant

SCENE: Ancient China

A BATTLE OF WITS

THE SETTING: *The traditional empty stage of the Chinese drama with the exception of a raised round section at stage right, not higher than three low steps, and not extending more than half-way down-stage. An entrance is made onto this upper level from stage right. Entrances are also at stage left, up-stage centre, and at right on stage level.*

At rise, PROPERTY MAN *is on upper right level just finishing the setting up of a long pole festooned with a few artificial leaves. As he finishes, he ambles down across stage to stand behind two chairs at left up-stage. There he remains in various relaxed attitudes as the play progresses or until his services are required.*

As PROPERTY MAN *ambles across the stage,* CHUNG TAI, *an elderly Chinese gentleman, richly dressed, enters from left. He strolls with a dignified air down-stage centre and looks directly out at the audience.*

CHUNG TAI (*with a bow*). It is the practice in the plays of my country to introduce oneself properly before taking part in the story. It is the custom and must, therefore, be correct. I, who have the honour to address you first, am Chung Tai, an official of the Court of the Emperor. My wife, of the Yu family, is a good woman as women go and over the years has dutifully presented me with four children. One of our children is a daughter, Silver Lotus, who has been married now these ten days. Our other child is a brave and handsome son now with the armies so gloriously repelling the Mongol invaders. Since a son who carries on the family name is three times better than a daughter, we have, as you will agree, four children. We consider ourselves blessed indeed.

> (CHUNG TAI *is finished with his introductory speech and so he simply turns his back and walks up-stage left where* PROPERTY MAN *provides him with a chair and he seats himself with dignity.*)

> (MADAM CHUNG *enters up-stage and comes directly down-stage, walking past* CHUNG TAI *as if he did not exist. She addresses the audience.*)

MADAM CHUNG. I am Madam Chung, wife of the Emperor's official. Today our newly-married daughter, Silver Lotus, returns to her home for the first time since her marriage. It is quite a ceremonial occasion and the whole house has been in an uproar all morning preparing for it. Now I shall greet my husband who is sitting in the garden enjoying the summer air. (*She turns as if seeing* CHUNG TAI *for the first time.*) Greetings, my husband.

CHUNG TAI (*rises and bows*). Greetings. Come and join me. The air is very fresh after all the cooking smells in the house.

MADAM CHUNG (*sits down wearily on a chair provided by* PROPERTY MAN, *to left of her husband*). We must have plenty to eat. It isn't every day a daughter returns from the first ten days of her marriage to pay respect to her parents.

CHUNG TAI. Has it been ten days? The older one gets, the more rapidly time seems to hustle one into the grave.

MADAM CHUNG (*musing*). I hope Silver Lotus is happy with her husband.

CHUNG TAI. Better hope she will be happy with her mother-in-law. It's the husband's mother who rules the household.

MADAM CHUNG. I hope the lady isn't the kind who shrieks for her cup of tea in the middle of the night.

CHUNG TAI. Silver Lotus will just have to endure it if she is. The young bride must wait upon her in-laws. It is the custom and must, therefore, be correct.

MADAM CHUNG. I might say that your own revered mother was always kind to me.

CHUNG TAI (*rises and bows*). Thank you. I take that as a great compliment to the spirit of my mother who will no doubt prick up her ears at a compliment like that.

MADAM CHUNG. She rarely beat me.

CHUNG TAI (*bows*). Thank you.

MADAM CHUNG. Rarely made me miss a meal.

CHUNG TAI (*bows*). Thank you.

MADAM CHUNG. And only roused me out of bed to bring her tea before dawn every second night or so.

CHUNG TAI (*bows*). Thank you. She was indeed a kind lady.

MADAM CHUNG. Very considerate of others.

CHUNG TAI. And myself? You have never said in all these years but I hope my character was always pleasing to you.

MADAM CHUNG (*with hesitation*). Yes.

CHUNG TAI. You're not very positive, I must say.

> (MADAM CHUNG *rises and goes to right, facing the steps. She bends her head and examines the steps carefully.*)

MADAM CHUNG. The flowers are lovely this year.

CHUNG TAI (*follows her and bends down, trying to see her face*). Will you tell me what it was that displeased you?

MADAM CHUNG. The peonies are budding well.

CHUNG TAI (*stands stiffly up*). I demand to know!

MADAM CHUNG (*turns slowly and faces him*). Only one thing. But I am just your wife and have no right to reprove you in any way.

CHUNG TAI. Quite correct; it is the custom. But I am *asking* you to tell me.

MADAM CHUNG. Well, then, you never took another wife, not even one.

CHUNG TAI. Oh—that.

MADAM CHUNG. I never complained. But it didn't seem quite wise to me at the time.

CHUNG TAI (*walks slowly back and sits down in his chair*). It is the custom and must, therefore, be correct. And yet I could never bring myself to do it. I don't know why.

MADAM CHUNG. It was embarrassing for me. People thought I was a domineering wife who exerted an influence beyond my right and refused to allow you to have another wife. When they thought that, they disliked me. Or, if they didn't think that, they thought worse. That you were not the man you might have been.

> (MADAM CHUNG *raises her sleeve until it almost covers her face.*)

CHUNG TAI. Oh, did they?

MADAM CHUNG.   And when they thought that, they were sorry for me.

CHUNG TAI.   Say no more. If I could turn time back thirty years, I would certainly take a second wife or a third or as many as would bring you happiness.

MADAM CHUNG   (*drops her sleeve*). How kind of you to think of it. It makes up for many years of inconvenience.

CHUNG TAI   (*bows*). You're welcome. It shows that it's best and wisest always to follow custom. Do you object to a little philosophy?

MADAM CHUNG.   You know my mind is not bent that way, but I will listen.

CHUNG TAI.   When wise men among us, out of their experience, have sifted away all intemperate and selfish courses, there remains that which is set down in the Classics as right behaviour. That is custom.

MADAM CHUNG.   Very prettily said. (CHUNG TAI *looks disappointed.*) And extremely clever.

CHUNG TAI   (*pleased*). Well, I know I'm not a man of original ideas but I have a good memory and that will get anybody through the finest university in the country. And I notice, too, that while I am on top the men of original ideas are far below striving foolishly against the tried and proven ways.

MADAM CHUNG.   You have always observed custom.

CHUNG TAI   (*raising his sleeve*). Except once.

MADAM CHUNG.   We'll never speak of that again.

CHUNG TAI   (*bows*). It's good of you to forget my shortcomings so soon.

MADAM CHUNG.   I try to be obedient.

(*Enter* ATTENDANT *on upper right level. He bows.*)

ATTENDANT. Silver Lotus approaches.

> (CHUNG TAI *and* MADAM CHUNG *rise as* ATTENDANT
> *exits. A pause. Enter* SILVER LOTUS *onto upper
> right level, a young and delicate Chinese lady of
> fifteen, beautifully and formally gowned.*)

SILVER LOTUS (*stepping forward and addressing the
audience*). I am Silver Lotus, only daughter to Chung Tai.
This is an auspicious day for me since I am paying my first
visit to my dear parents since my marriage. It is the custom
to come on the tenth day and, although I have little respect
for custom as such, I am happy to be here.

> (SILVER LOTUS *now turns to her parents and kneels
> gracefully before them.*)

Silver Lotus respectfully greets her father.

> (*She kotows to him, touching her brow lightly to the
> ground.*)

Silver Lotus respectfully greets her mother.

> (*She kotows to her mother.*)

CHUNG TAI. Enough of ceremony. Come to your father.

MADAM CHUNG. And to your mother.

> (SILVER LOTUS *hurries down the steps and they both
> envelop her at once in fond embrace.*)

CHUNG TAI. My dear daughter.

MADAM CHUNG. Dearest one.

SILVER LOTUS. My dear parents.

CHUNG TAI (*suddenly breaking away; loudly*). Silver
Lotus!

> (MADAM CHUNG *and* SILVER LOTUS *break apart.*)

SILVER LOTUS. Yes, Father?

(CHUNG TAI *raises his arm slowly so that by the time he finishes his question his face is hidden.*)

CHUNG TAI.   Have you observed the proprieties in entering your old home?

SILVER LOTUS.   You may confidently lower your sleeve, Father. I have observed all the proprieties.

MADAM CHUNG.   My daughter.

CHUNG TAI.   You have made obeisance to the Household deities?

SILVER LOTUS.   Yes, Father.

CHUNG TAI.   And made suitable offerings?

SILVER LOTUS.   I have given sweetmeats and burned the incense which my husband provided for my visit. He was anxious that everything be done properly.

MADAM CHUNG.   And does your husband please you?

SILVER LOTUS   (*goes to right*).   How lovely the rockery is this season.

CHUNG TAI.   Just like her mother.

(SILVER LOTUS *makes her way up the steps in a winding manner as if walking up a pathway.*)

SILVER LOTUS.   I believe it's lovelier than last year.

MADAM CHUNG.   It is, no doubt. But other things in nature interest us more today.

(*At this point,* CHUNG TAI *signals* PROPERTY MAN *to bring a chair. The* PROPERTY MAN *is busy lounging in one of the chairs smoking his pipe and does not see him.*)

CHUNG TAI   (*to the women*).   Just a minute, please.
(*To* PROPERTY MAN.) Hey you there! (*shouts*) You! Bring me a chair!

(PROPERTY MAN *jumps up and hurriedly brings a chair forward.*)

Don't you know this play? Watch yourself from now on!

(CHUNG TAI *sits as* PROPERTY MAN *sheepishly returns to his post and manages to remain alert for some time.*)

(*To the women.*) All right.

MADAM CHUNG.   Other things in nature interest us more than the rockery today.

SILVER LOTUS.   Yes, I expect so.

MADAM CHUNG.   Namely, how does your husband please you?

SILVER LOTUS.   With all respect, my dear mother, is that a proper question? It isn't for him to please me, but for me to please him.

CHUNG TAI   (*laughs*).

MADAM CHUNG   (*silences him with a look*).   You sound just like your father. Answer a plain question, please.

SILVER LOTUS.   You have suspected, I'm sure, that I have read a good many romantic novels.

MADAM CHUNG.   I suspect no such thing.

SILVER LOTUS.   I always meant to tell you but my memory is so bad for things like that. I have often spent time just at the break of dawn when all the birds were singing to greet the sun, sitting in my chamber and reading those glorious stories of romance and tears and happiness.

MADAM CHUNG.   How was it possible?

SILVER LOTUS.   They are such tiny books to hide in a sleeve or under a pillow. Not at all like the Classics which are endless and boring. In fact, the more interesting a book is the shorter it seems to be. It's very unfair.

MADAM CHUNG. What has all this to do with your husband?

SILVER LOTUS (*quietly*). He is, no doubt, according to the world, a fine husband. I don't deny it because opinion is against me. Still—not one of the heroes in my romantic books was quite so—fat. And since I had never seen him before my wedding day and had such little knowledge of the real world, I wasn't quite prepared.

CHUNG TAI. Your heroes weren't so rich either, I'll be bound.

SILVER LOTUS. No, they lived on air—and love.

CHUNG TAI
and   } (*shocked*). Love!
MADAM CHUNG

SILVER LOTUS. I'm not sure what love is, but that's what they lived on.

MADAM CHUNG. I must sit down!

(PROPERTY MAN *promptly provides a chair, with a fearful glance at* CHUNG TAI *who loftily ignores him.*)

(SILVER LOTUS *comes down the winding path and stands by their chairs.*)

SILVER LOTUS. Have I said the wrong thing?

CHUNG TAI. Love is not the custom.

MADAM CHUNG. Then you aren't inclined to your husband. I can't understand it. Your surnames were right for each other.

CHUNG TAI. We were scrupulous on that point. He is fire and you are wood and, according to the astrologers, that is favourable. Very.

MADAM CHUNG. And the diviner who fixed the wedding date is said to be infallible at choosing lucky days.

CHUNG TAI. With all these tried practices in accord, it must be you who are wrong, Silver Lotus.

SILVER LOTUS. I am *not* wrong.

MADAM CHUNG. What a way to speak!

SILVER LOTUS (*raises her sleeve*). I apologize. I know I am wrong a good deal.

CHUNG TAI. I'm surprised at you, Silver Lotus. You've always been a sensible, realistic girl.

SILVER LOTUS. I *do* appreciate his money, Father. It is comforting, despite everything else.

CHUNG TAI. Remember you're grown up now. You'll be sixteen in November. What will people think if they find you live in a dream world and act like a child?

SILVER LOTUS. I know. I'm sorry. (*She weeps.*) But —he is a—brute!

(SILVER LOTUS *turns away to the back and cries in her sleeve.*)

CHUNG TAI. It seems that in spite of all we've done, our daughter isn't happy after all.

MADAM CHUNG. She's crying so hard—it doesn't seem like the formal crying relatives use at a funeral—and she has said such rash things, that I'm forced to agree with you.

CHUNG TAI. It's too bad.

MADAM CHUNG. But unalterable.

CHUNG TAI. Yes, unalterable. Still we must try to console her. (*Calls.*) Silver Lotus!

SILVER LOTUS (*coming back, drying her eyes*). Your obedient daughter.

CHUNG TAI. You know the old saying: That which cannot be altered must be endured. Do you not see hope in that?

SILVER LOTUS. I see hope in *some* things.

MADAM CHUNG. Please explain yourself.

SILVER LOTUS. My husband is brutal. There is hope in that.

MADAM CHUNG. What do you mean by that?

CHUNG TAI. She means he will have enemies, I think.

SILVER LOTUS. And he is fat. It is often said that fat is a strain on the heart.

MADAM CHUNG. You don't mean to tell me you wish your husband dead?

SILVER LOTUS. I wouldn't say such a thing. It's the sign of a bad character to wish another person's death.

MADAM CHUNG. Oh, these meaningless generalizations. (*To* CHUNG TAI.) They are your fault.

CHUNG TAI. *My* fault?

MADAM CHUNG. Isn't it from you that she's heard them all her life?

CHUNG TAI. I can't help that. I'm a statesman.

(ATTENDANT *enters from up-stage centre.*)

ATTENDANT. His Excellent Magistrate, Sun Chu.

CHUNG TAI (*rising quickly*). It is Sun Chu, here on business. Have tea prepared, please.

MADAM CHUNG. I'll see to it.

(*Exit* MADAM CHUNG, *left.*)

CHUNG TAI (*to* SILVER LOTUS). Retire a little, but not far. He will want to greet you on this ceremonial occasion.

(*Enter* SUN CHU, *a young and handsome man of slender build, modestly but expensively attired.*)

(SILVER LOTUS *makes her way slowly up the winding path to stand by the pole as* SUN CHU *bows to the audience and speaks to them.*)

SUN CHU. Your servant, Sun Chu. I am, it is true, a young man but I am cutting quite a figure as a magistrate hereabouts. There has recently been trouble with tax evaders and I have come to consult with Chung Tai, who was a great friend of my father, to see if something can't be done on a higher level. I hold the law in great esteem and, although I never pay taxes myself, it seems unsafe and rebellious to me when others seek this same privilege.

> (SUN CHU *now bows to* CHUNG TAI *who has stood motionless throughout his speech.*)

CHUNG TAI (*saluting him*). Welcome, Magistrate Sun.

SUN CHU. Thank you, sir. It's good to see you again.

CHUNG TAI. God rest the spirit of your father who was my best friend.

SUN CHU (*bows*). I thank you.

CHUNG TAI. I'm glad to see you again on such a happy day. Our dear daughter has just returned for the first traditional visit home since her marriage.

> (CHUNG TAI *signals to her and* SILVER LOTUS *slowly retraces her steps carefully down the winding pathway.*)

SUN CHU. I have been away. I had no idea——

CHUNG TAI. We have made her a good match.

SUN CHU. Naturally. You have my congratulations.

CHUNG TAI. Our thanks. She has married a splendid husband and is glad as a girl can be.

> (SILVER LOTUS *comes modestly up to them and looks shyly at* SUN CHU.)

SILVER LOTUS. I was just looking at my old tree, Father. (*She points to the pole.*) I used to play under it as a child. What joyful times we all had then.

(SILVER LOTUS *bows to* SUN CHU.)

SUN CHU.   Silver Lotus is more beautiful than ever.

SILVER LOTUS.   It is happiness.

SUN CHU.   The tone is sadness.

CHUNG TAI.   The reason is modesty.

SILVER LOTUS.   My smile always vanishes at dusk. I am always sad at dusk, when the day passes away and the night is coming.

CHUNG TAI.   What a sensitive child.

SILVER LOTUS.   No. I am grown up now and if I act like a child at my age heaven knows what people will think of me. You said so only a while ago, Father.

CHUNG TAI.   Watch this girl, Sun Chu. She's a hard bargainer and never forgets a thing. What a future she would have if she were a man.

SUN CHU.   It's too bad.

CHUNG TAI.   But unalterable.

SILVER LOTUS.   I've outwitted a man before now. That's some satisfaction.

SUN CHU.   I have cause to know it.

SILVER LOTUS.   You have.

SUN CHU.   And I have never forgotten my pledge.

CHUNG TAI.   What are you two talking about?

SUN CHU.   Sir, many years ago, when my father, on business of state, would come to visit you, I would come with him. As you and he became engrossed in your affairs, Silver Lotus and I would quietly steal from the house and play together in the garden.

CHUNG TAI.   I didn't know that.

SILVER LOTUS.   There have been times when I have outwitted even you, Father.

SUN CHU. We played many games, some simple, some complex, but though I was six years older than Silver Lotus, she always outwitted me, gained the advantage and came out the victor.

SILVER LOTUS. Of course we were only children.

SUN CHU. But I remember my pledge then to outwit you one day.

(*Enter* ATTENDANT *up-stage centre.*)

ATTENDANT. Tea is served! Tea is served!

(*Exit* ATTENDANT.)

CHUNG TAI. Tea is ready, Magistrate, and I imagine the guests have begun to arrive for the celebration. You will surely stay and join the festivities.

SUN CHU. I would be honoured.

(CHUNG TAI *moves towards up-stage centre.* SILVER LOTUS *and* SUN CHU *linger behind.*)

SILVER LOTUS. See how our tree stands against the fading light.

SUN CHU. Our lives have changed since we played beneath it.

SILVER LOTUS. I wish I were still a child. I wish it! I wish it!

SUN CHU (*lightly*). So that you could still outwit me?

SILVER LOTUS (*throwing off depression*). Oh yes, I like a battle of wits, don't you?

SUN CHU. I do.

CHUNG TAI (*turns and looks at them*). Come along. It is always best and safest to obey established customs. And a married woman should not speak over-long with a widowed man.

(CHUNG TAI *goes slowly through the exit and disappears.* SUN CHU *and* SILVER LOTUS *follow. As*
SILVER LOTUS *reaches the exit, she turns and waves
to the pole, her tree.*)

SILVER LOTUS.   Goodnight, my tree.

(*They go.*)

(*For a moment, the stage is empty except for* PROP-
ERTY MAN *who is now nearly asleep in one of the
chairs.*)

(*Enter* ATTENDANT *from left. He hurries to stage
centre and quickly walks with long strides for three
complete circles in a clockwise direction. His last
circular motion brings him facing the audience.*)

ATTENDANT.   Three months have passed and we find
ourselves in a cell of his Imperial Majesty's local jail. Why
we are here will be presently unfolded.

(*He exits, up-stage centre.*)

(*Enter* WORKER *from left as if pushed with great force
from behind. He is half naked and wears old
trousers and sandals. His arms are tied behind his
back. As he hurtles on-stage he falls on his knees.*)

WORKER.   Oh, God, that I was ever born. (*To audience.*)
I beg your pardon. (*He rises painfully.*) I'm all upset and
I forgot you were there. (*Pulling himself together.*) I prefer
not to tell you my name. It is of no importance and now
I am here in jail the less it is known the better for my poor
family. Even a lowly worker's family can feel disgrace. I
dread to think of their feelings when they see the red notice
posted with my humble name followed by: "hanged" or
"beheaded" or "burned" or whichever way they do it.

(*A sound of a clanging door is heard off.*)

VOICE (*off*). He's in there, sir.

SUN CHU (*off*). Thank you.

WORKER. I hear somebody coming. These last hours have taught me that it's best to be in a humble attitude when anyone approaches because, if you're not, they'll soon shove you into one and it's very hard on the knee-caps. If you'll excuse me.

(*He sinks gently to his knees, bows his head and is perfectly still as* SUN CHU *blusters in from left.*)

SUN CHU (*shouting*). Is this the wretch?

(*He faces the left entrance and shouts at the top of his voice.*)

Wretch! Guilty Wretch! Villain! Guard, go and leave him to me.

VOICE (*off*). Yes, sir.

(*The clanging door is heard once more.*)

SUN CHU (*relaxing*). Well, he's gone. (*Looks around.*) What a miserable hole of a cell. Are there no chairs even?

(PROPERTY MAN, *who has been aroused by this clamour, supplies* SUN CHU *with a chair which is placed close to the* WORKER *who has remained kneeling and motionless throughout.*)

Now, sir, what have you to say for yourself?

(*There is no reply, except for a tremor of fear.*)

(*gently*) Come now, I only shouted for effect. It's part of my job. The guards, you know, will report my attitude to the warden, who will report it to the governor, who will report it to the Minister of Justice, who will report at the quarter to the Emperor who, very likely in this Festival season, will mention it to the Deity. So you can see, I had no choice. Harshness and arrogance are expected from a man in my position.

WORKER (*mumbling*). Yes, sir.

SUN CHU. Nothing personal. I am a man, like yourself.

WORKER. Yes, sir.

SUN CHU. I want to hear all about this business. (*Pause, no answer.*) Come on, nobody can be so spiritless he doesn't want to tell his side of a story.

WORKER (*looks slowly up*). Abjectness is expected from a man in my position.

SUN CHU. Well, we have played our respective roles long enough. Now I want the facts.

WORKER. May I stand, sir? My knees.

SUN CHU. Certainly you may.

WORKER (*rises, stretches his legs*). I'm only a worthless proletarian, sir, but I'm not used to much kneeling nevertheless.

(SUN CHU *makes a gesture of impatience.*)

Yes, sir, facts. The facts are these. As you probably know, sir, there is a bad shortage of firewood in this district. The lower brush and branches have been cleared out long ago and it takes an energetic man to get the high wood. Up to three months ago, I was a bird-seller, sir, but what with the depression, luxury trade fell off and things looked black. So, I say to myself, what can I sell that people have got to have? Wood, I say. So I dropped my bird-hawking and took to gathering wood. And it didn't turn out badly, until this morning, that is.

SUN CHU. So that is what you were doing up in the tree, is it?

WORKER. Yes, sir. You see that tree outside the window, sir?

> (WORKER *indicates to right of* SUN CHU *with his head;* SUN CHU *turns and looks in that direction.*)

SUN CHU. I do.

WORKER. It was a tree much like that, sir. Very spreading and broad-like. The trunk was partly split by lightning and there was plenty of good dead wood at the top, too. Enough for a day's sales, I figured, so up I climbed.

SUN CHU. When did you see the man?

WORKER. As I was just getting ready to work on a branch, he came into the woods from the road.

SUN CHU. You didn't entice him in?

WORKER. No, sir, I swear I didn't.

SUN CHU. Then why should such a man come into the woods at all?

WORKER. Well, sir, for very private reasons, that might prompt anybody to look for a bit of privacy—uh—for a few moments. Very private, very natural reasons, sir. We've all been in the situation at some time, no doubt.

SUN CHU. I see. And you claim he stopped right beneath your tree—for these private reasons?

WORKER. He *did,* sir. And after he'd gone to so much trouble looking around to be sure he was private, I didn't have the rudeness to make a noise, so I clung to my branch as silent as a little bird.

SUN CHU. Don't report poetically. It only confuses things.

WORKER. I'm sorry, sir. Well, there I was, clinging to that branch when along comes an evil spirit and, spying a perfect set-up for devilment, he cuts the branch I was clinging to and down I falls on that unsuspecting innocent man and the blow kills him then and there. If he hadn't been so well buttered with fat, I would have been killed, too.

SUN CHU.   So that's your story. (*He rises.*) That it was an evil spirit wandering through the woods who spitefully cut the branch and brought on disaster?

WORKER.   Yes, sir.

SUN CHU.   Tell me. Why do you say it was an evil spirit?

WORKER.   Because it's common knowledge the woods are full of them.

SUN CHU.   Not to protect yourself and escape the blame?

WORKER.   Oh, no. No! It was a spirit!

SUN CHU.   Do you think I believe in spirits?

WORKER.   I don't know, sir. I only know they exist and work evil among men. I carry charms against them all the time.

SUN CHU.   Then why didn't your charms frighten this particular evil spirit away?

WORKER.   Well, sir, it may be one of those black unlucky days when there's so much against the luck of a man that nothing he can do turns it away.

SUN CHU (*strolls away a little, thinking*).   Hmmmm. That's interesting. Interesting.

WORKER.   You're—thinking—sir?

SUN CHU.   I am. I'm thinking that it's good for you that you claim an evil spirit is the agent of this business.

WORKER.   I do. I know it. It's true.

SUN CHU.   I have no doubt you believe it, too. Now many a man in your position would have told me that this tragedy was an accident, that the branch was rotten, or some other such nonsense which would only prove him guilty. But you, a natural, unspoiled, obedient vassal of the state plead an evil spirit. It is men like you who do not interfere with natural superstition who keep government stable and worthy men like myself in power. For no matter what disaster befalls the nation I've no doubt you're quite willing to lay it at the door of your evil spirits, holding no government and no official to blame.

WORKER. Oh, I wouldn't hold any human to blame, sir. We're all at the mercy of the spirits.

SUN CHU. Good. I don't think we can let you die. It may take a day or two—red tape, you know—but I'll soon have you back to your haunted woods and your wood-gathering.

WORKER. I may go back to birds, sir.

SUN CHU. As you wish. Either way, you will be free to spread the gospel. (*Calls.*) Guard! Guard!

VOICE (*off*). Yes, sir.

SUN CHU. Unlock the gate.

VOICE (*off*). Yes, sir.

> (*Sound of gate clanging open.* WORKER *falls to his knees.*)

SUN CHU. Put this man into a more comfortable cell and make sure he has his lunch.

> (SUN CHU *exits,* WORKER *rises and addresses the audience.*)

WORKER. I had no idea it was so wise to be ignorant.

VOICE (*off*). Come on, you.

WORKER. Yes, sir, with pleasure, sir.

> (WORKER *goes, left.*)

ATTENDANT (*appears up-stage, centre, bawls out his words*). The garden of the Emperor's official, Chung Tai.

(*He exits.*)

(SILVER LOTUS *enters onto upper level, right and, descending the winding pathway, comes down-stage and addresses the audience.*)

SILVER LOTUS.   Three months have passed since my first visit to my parental home after my marriage. This after-noon they sent for me urgently but when I arrived would tell me nothing. Now they have shooed me out here into the garden with much mystery and whispering between them. I can tell something is going on, but since no one seems pre-pared to say what it is, I will enjoy the colouring of the flowers until they are.

(*She turns back to the steps and examines the in-visible rockery, singing a quiet, wordless and tranquil song as she does. Continues during fol-lowing.*)

(*Enter* SUN CHU *up-stage centre. He comes quickly down-stage and speaks to the audience.*)

SUN CHU.   I have hurried to Chung Tai's peaceful garden to bring Silver Lotus news of her husband's death. Her father and mother are reluctant to tell her as they know what a sad blow it will be. However, it must be done. Silver Lotus.

(*He turns and approaches* SILVER LOTUS.)

Silver Lotus.

SILVER LOTUS.   Sun Chu. You! I must retire.

SUN CHU.   Don't go.

SILVER LOTUS.   We shouldn't be alone. It's not proper.

SUN CHU.   Your good parents sent me to you.

SILVER LOTUS.   Didn't Father say: It is not the custom; therefore, it is not correct?

SUN CHU. Not this time. No. (*Pause.*) I have come to bring you news. (*Pause.*) Don't you want to know what it is?

SILVER LOTUS. I would like to know first what *kind* of news it is. Is it good news, or bad?

SUN CHU. I'm afraid it's bad.

SILVER LOTUS. Then it would be best to forget you have any news at all and we will simply admire the blooms. Aren't the chrysanthemums beautiful, Sun Chu?

SUN CHU. You aren't very curious.

SILVER LOTUS. I always am about good news. Not about bad.

SUN CHU. You'll have to hear it eventually. It can't be avoided.

SILVER LOTUS. Then if, in addition, you won't admire the chrysanthemums with me, I suppose you may as well tell me now.

SUN CHU. I—I——

SILVER LOTUS. What's the matter?

SUN CHU. There must be a way of breaking bad news without *saying* it.

SILVER LOTUS. You could write to me about it. Write to me about it some time next week. That would be better.

SUN CHU. No, I must say it. The truth is—your husband is dead.

SILVER LOTUS (*astounded*). My—husband? Did you —say—dead?

(*Enter* CHUNG TAI *and* MADAM CHUNG *from up-stage. They hurry to* SILVER LOTUS.)

SUN CHU. I'm sorry.

SILVER LOTUS. Oh, I can't think! My—husband. Dead.

But he was in good health at breakfast this morning and complained about everything just as usual. *How* did he die?

SUN CHU. He was killed by a falling man.

SILVER LOTUS. A falling man?

SUN CHU. A wood-gatherer. He fell out of a tree in the woods. Your husband happened to be under the tree.

SILVER LOTUS. What was he doing in the woods?

SUN CHU. Oh—uh—he was writing a poem. A poem to nature's enjoyments. That should be a consolation to you; to know his mind was occupied with aesthetic matters in his last moments.

SILVER LOTUS. Oh, Father! Mother!

CHUNG TAI (*embracing her*). Poor, dear daughter.

MADAM CHUNG (*embracing her*). Take courage, my dear.

SILVER LOTUS. Father, you always know the correct proceeding in every situation. I'm not much practised in becoming a widow. What should I do now?

CHUNG TAI. I think you should cry.

SILVER LOTUS. Then I shall.

> (SILVER LOTUS *goes a little up-stage where* PROPERTY MAN *supplies her with a huge handkerchief into which she forces her sobs.*)

CHUNG TAI. What a disaster. I don't know what we've done to deserve this.

MADAM CHUNG. Poor Silver Lotus. I've brought her up so carefully. But now, as a widow, what standing will she have, what rights? None, none! She'll be nothing but a slave to her mother-in-law with no hope in the world for anything better. All my work was for nothing.

SILVER LOTUS (*a huge sob*). Now, I'm *really* crying.

SUN CHU. Weren't you before?

SILVER LOTUS. No.

SUN CHU. But your dear husband is dead.

SILVER LOTUS. He was my husband, but he wasn't dear. He was a brute.

CHUNG TAI (*shocked*). Silver Lotus; your real feelings are a family matter.

SILVER LOTUS. The shock has made me truthful. I hated him.

MADAM CHUNG. Oh, enough of honesty! It's quite uncalled-for.

SILVER LOTUS. And yet without him, I'll be nothing but a slave to a cranky old woman who beats me and makes me bring her cups of tea in the middle of the night. I'm not permitted by law to return to my father's house and I have no independent means. Oh, it's hopeless.

MADAM CHUNG. Come, my dear, don't think of it now. Come and rest awhile first.

SILVER LOTUS. Yes, Mother, that would be best. And I may have a little something to eat. All this emotion has made me hungry.

(MADAM CHUNG *and* SILVER LOTUS *in close and comforting conversation, exit slowly up-stage.*)

CHUNG TAI. Come, Sun Chu, there's nothing to be done. The position of a widowed woman is pitiable indeed. (*Wearily.*) Still, it is decreed by custom and must, therefore, be correct.

SUN CHU. I am beginning to wonder.

(*They exit down-stage, right. As they go,* PROPERTY MAN *brings forward a small black table and places it down-stage, centre. He then brings two chairs,*

*placing one at each side of the table. He then
resumes his usual place.*)

(*Enter* SILVER LOTUS *from left. She speaks to the
audience.*)

SILVER LOTUS.   It is now two weeks since the burial of
my husband and, day by day, my position grows intolerable.
But I have a plan and since Sun Chu is the Magistrate and
a man of power, I have asked him to come and speak to
me over a cup of wine. I have made discreet inquiries and
I believe I see a way to alleviate my position a little, although
I must be harsh in order to bring it about.

(*She goes to one of the chairs and sits perfectly still
during the following.*)

(*Enter* SUN CHU *from right. He speaks to the
audience.*)

SUN CHU.   I have been asked to attend Silver Lotus here
in the garden. I wonder what she is up to? My feeling is
that she is ready to resume our battle of wits.

(*He approaches* SILVER LOTUS *and bows.*)

SUN CHU.   Greetings, Silver Lotus.

SILVER LOTUS.   Let's not be ceremonious. But sit down
and have a cup of wine.

SUN CHU.   Thank you.

(*He lifts an imaginary cup from the table and drinks.*)

SILVER LOTUS.   It is one of my father's best wines.

SUN CHU.   It is delicious.

(*He drinks again.*)

SILVER LOTUS.   Sun Chu, the circumstances of my husband's death were strange and unfortunate, doesn't it seem
to you?

SUN CHU. Certainly unusual and certainly unfortunate.

SILVER LOTUS. And my own circumstances are now worse than before. I feel a certain emotion rising in my heart.

SUN CHU (*eagerly*). What—emotion is that?

SILVER LOTUS. Revenge!

SUN CHU. Oh.

SILVER LOTUS. I have asked my father about it. He has consulted his books and says that, in law, I am in the right to demand the death of my husband's slayer.

SUN CHU. But the man did not intend to kill your husband. It was an accident.

SILVER LOTUS. He was the agent of my husband's death. I believe that is how the law puts it. And I have a right— intent or no intent—to demand his death in forfeit.

SUN CHU. But even if you have, what good would that be to you?

SILVER LOTUS. Invaluable good. It would raise me high in the estimation of my mother-in-law, who feels her son's death very deeply. If I seek and get revenge she will not be so cruel to me.

SUN CHU. That is a sound answer. I always agree, in principle, with self-interest. Still, I can't permit it.

SILVER LOTUS. And why not? What is this obscure wood-gatherer to you?

SUN CHU. He is much to me. I am a man who sees symbols in things. I have a first-rate imagination, as you may have noticed, and this simple wood-gatherer repre-sents to me the ideal of the obedient and servile citizen who keeps conservatives like me and your father in our proper high positions in the world. The safety of the state depends upon such people. And in these rebellious times not even one of them can be sacrificed.

SILVER LOTUS. But if I *demand* his execution?

SUN CHU (*thinking hard*). Hmmmm. Well.

SILVER LOTUS. As Magistrate you have no choice but to see the righteousness of my cause.

SUN CHU (*rises*). You have thought this out well.

SILVER LOTUS. Our battle of wits seems to be going my way again.

SUN CHU. "As Magistrate" is the phrase which keeps sounding in my brain. "As Magistrate".

SILVER LOTUS (*pleased with herself*). As Magistrate.

SUN CHU (*crisply*). You are right. I have no choice.

SILVER LOTUS. Then, clearly, he must die.

SUN CHU. Clearly, he must. However, *as Magistrate,* I have one privilege.

SILVER LOTUS. What is that?

SUN CHU. That of fixing upon the manner of execution. What method would you suggest?

SILVER LOTUS. Oh, I am not of a cruel disposition. I would have no opinion.

SUN CHU. It would be only just, surely, if he were to die in the same way your husband met his end.

SILVER LOTUS. I suppose so.

SUN CHU. And, as Magistrate, it is my duty to choose the instrument.

SILVER LOTUS. No doubt, but all these details are immaterial to me.

SUN CHU. I don't think you will find them immaterial because, as Magistrate, I have just decided that the instrument of death will be—Silver Lotus.

SILVER LOTUS (*rising in agitation*). Me? But that's absurd.

SUN CHU. It's really quite easy. You simply fall out of a tree onto the wood-gatherer's head and kill him just as he killed your husband.

SILVER LOTUS. But that's impossible.

SUN CHU. Oh, not at all. We'll tie him down. You can't miss.

SILVER LOTUS. But *I* might be killed.

SUN CHU. Then what more glorious way to die than swooping down on the air like an avenging spirit to destroy your husband's killer. You will become a saint!

SILVER LOTUS. Tell me truthfully—we have always been truthful with each other—can you do this?

SUN CHU. I can.

SILVER LOTUS (*sobs in her sleeve*). Then I am lost.

SUN CHU. Not so. I have some news for you. (*Pause.*) Are you not curious?

SILVER LOTUS. What kind of news is it? Good news or bad news?

SUN CHU. It is good news.

SILVER LOTUS. Then I am curious.

SUN CHU. I, too, have made inquiries about your position and I find that, like most mothers-in-law, yours is a very greedy woman.

SILVER LOTUS. Oh, how right that is. She eats like a pig.

SUN CHU. And so, this very day, I have sent my emissary to her.

SILVER LOTUS. Your emissary?

SUN CHU. Mine. And he has paid her a sum which even your father could not afford and which she gobbled up so fast that she very nearly choked.

SILVER LOTUS. But—why have you done this?

SUN CHU. So that I might free you and ask your father, although it is not the custom, if you might marry me. As you may know, the wife my parents chose for me died a year ago and I am, as you may have guessed, a lonely man.

SILVER LOTUS. But my father?

SUN CHU. He has consented.

SILVER LOTUS. It is—not—the custom.

SUN CHU. No.

SILVER LOTUS. For a widow to re-marry. It is—not—the custom.

SUN CHU. No.

SILVER LOTUS (*slowly*). But I have never cared over-much for custom.

SUN CHU. No.

SILVER LOTUS. And it would offend my sense of form to see all your beautiful plans ruined.

(*She turns towards him and* SUN CHU *embraces her, a very formal and correct embrace.*)

(*Enter* CHUNG TAI *and* MADAM CHUNG *up-stage.*)

MADAM CHUNG. Dear Silver Lotus.

CHUNG TAI. I'm not sure I approve now that I see a widow and a widower embracing.

MADAM CHUNG. Of course you approve.

SUN CHU. And we promise to observe scrupulously every custom from now on to make up for this bad beginning. We will, for instance, show every deference to our parents.

(SILVER LOTUS *and* SUN CHU *bow deeply to* CHUNG TAI *and* MADAM CHUNG.)

CHUNG TAI and MADAM CHUNG. } Thank you.

SILVER LOTUS.   Dear husband-to-be, why, if all this was arranged, did you let me go on about my own harmless scheme to better my position?

SUN CHU.   Because I had to win our battle of wits. Otherwise, you would have been impossible to live with in all the years ahead.

SILVER LOTUS.   For once, I'm glad to have lost. To lose just this one important battle of wits seems very clever of me.

SUN CHU.   It does.

CHUNG TAI.   Well, let's go inside. It's getting too cold to be out in the garden. And tea is waiting.

MADAM CHUNG.   We have broken enough precedent for one day. I suggest we go in formally and court proper procedure again.

CHUNG TAI.   A splendid idea. It is the custom and must, therefore, be correct.

> (*And so they follow custom.* CHUNG TAI *is in front with* MADAM CHUNG *a little behind.* SUN CHU *follows with* SILVER LOTUS *behind as is proper with betrothed couples. The first three make a slow and stately exit, up-stage. As* SILVER LOTUS *reaches the exit, she turns and raises her hand in a salute to her tree.*)

SILVER LOTUS.   Goodbye, my tree. We shall have lovely times together soon again.

> (*Before she turns and goes,* PROPERTY MAN *comes forward, takes the little table under one arm and, dragging a chair across the floor with the other, wanders towards back left as the curtain falls.*)

ROYAL SUSPECT

by

YVONNE FIRKINS

CHARACTERS

Madame Sidonie

Marie

Landlord

His Wife

Mayor

Governor

Anton

A Passing Traveller

His Secretary

Younger Maid

Older Maid

Gaston

A Gendarme

Citizens

SCENE: A village inn on the main road from Paris to
the Swiss Frontier

TIME: The year 1791. A winter evening about 9 p.m.

ROYAL SUSPECT

SCENE: *The main room of a wayside inn. It is a room giving the impression of being well used, with dark heavy wooden doors and window frames. A broad low window takes up most of the back wall. It has heavily leaded panes, and, as the night is black and stormy, nothing can be seen outside. Standing in front of the window is an old wooden seat or chest.*

Up right are two steps leading to a hallway in which is the door to an outside courtyard. (This door need not be visible, but if it is seen from the front, it should appear to be of heavy wood with large iron latches and locks of the period.)

Stage right is a broad stone fireplace with a wooden mantel on which stand two brass or iron candlesticks with candles. The candles are unlighted.

A wooden stool or high-backed chair stands at each corner of the hearth, and a backless bench is directly in front of it. A fire is burning in the hearth, just enough to throw a faint glow over the room before the candles are lit.

Up left is a wooden staircase of about six steps with a heavy-looking balustrade. This leads to a landing which goes off left to the upstairs interior. A long serving-table stands beneath the side of the staircase. On it are tankards and appropriate dishes. Left centre of the stage is the large dining-table—preferably round—with four or five chairs round it, and a large double candlestick in the centre.

When the curtain rises, the only light on the stage is the flickering glow of the firelight. The general atmosphere is one of warmth and shelter from the storm raging outside.

There are sounds of wind and rain before the curtain rises. These continue with variations, conditioned by the opening and closing of the outside door up right, during the action of the play. They should be sufficiently subdued not to dominate the dialogue, and should be almost imperceptible by the end of the play. There is no one on stage at the rise of the curtain. The only apparent source of light is the glow of the fire. There is a faint sound of wind and rain from outside, and then the sound of horses' hoofs and coach wheels as though on the cobbled stones of a yard. A moment later there is a rap on the door up right, a pause, and then more raps. The LANDLORD *enters down left. He is carrying a lighted candle and a large taper. As he crosses toward the table, there is a series of loud impatient raps on the door. The* LANDLORD *lights the taper from the candle he is carrying, then lights the two candles on the centre table, calling as he does so:*

LANDLORD. Yes, yes, gentlemen—coming—coming.

> (*He goes to the door up right, opens it, and is brushed aside by* MADAME *who rushes past him into the room. He turns to follow her.*)

Your pardon, Madame (*He bows.*), for keeping you waiting. I thought it was the young gentleman from the Château.

> (*He approaches her, holding the candle higher as though to see her face more clearly, but the hood of* MADAME's *cloak is drawn well over her face, and in the light of the candle her features are barely discernible.*)

MADAME (*speaking hurriedly as though excited. Her voice is extremely attractive*). It is really no matter—Oh, what a night! Are you the innkeeper?

LANDLORD. At your service, Madame.

MADAME. We would like to break our journey here for a little while; it is impossible to go any further in this vile weather without resting the horses. (*She suddenly dashes back to the door up right and calls.*) Come along, Marie, and bring the cloaks and rugs with you.

> (*The LANDLORD lights the candles on the mantel over the fireplace.*)

MADAME (*coming back into the room, and pushing the hood back up from her face*). We would like to rest here for a while, please, my maid and me. Can you provide us with some supper, and send a man to help the coachman with the horses?

> (*As she talks, MADAME moves over to the fireplace and stands at the up-stage end of the seat before the fire. The LANDLORD has moved down to light the last candle on the mantel, and he turns to face MADAME with a broad smile of pleasure at having such a beautiful guest.*)

LANDLORD. We will do our best, Madame. Ah, here comes my good wife. She will look after you.

> (*The WIFE appears in the doorway of the kitchen down left. Immediately behind her is the YOUNG MAIDSERVANT.*)

MADAME (*turning to warm her hands before the fire*). Thank you.

> (*The WIFE comes forward just as MARIE enters up right with her arms full of wraps and bundles.*)

MARIE.   There is some baggage in the coach, Madame.
Would it not be best to have it brought inside?

LANDLORD   (*to* MAIDSERVANT *who is still standing in the
doorway down left*). Go and get Georges.

>   (MAID *exits*. WIFE *goes to* MARIE *and helps her to
>   put things on the window seat.* MADAME, *still
>   warming herself before the fire, turns repeatedly
>   to look towards the door up right as though listen-
>   ing for something.* LANDLORD *crosses and lights
>   candle on serving-table, left.* GEORGES, *the handy-
>   man, enters down left followed by* YOUNG MAID-
>   SERVANT.)

LANDLORD.   Georges, bring in the ladies' baggage from
the coach.

GEORGES   (*touching his forelock*). Yes, master.

>   (GEORGES *exits up right.* LANDLORD *moves to the door
>   up right to watch Georges with the baggage.*)

WIFE   (*crossing to* MADAME). Won't you sit down and
get warm, Madame? (*To* MAID *who is standing down left.*)
Suzanne, go and see the upstairs rooms are ready for
Madame. She will need a rest before travelling again on
a night like this.

>   (MAID *curtseys and exits up left.*)

MADAME   (*sitting on bench before fire down-stage*).
Thank you very much.

WIFE   (*going to* MADAME). Shall I take your cloak,
Madame? (*She goes to lift it from* MADAME'*s shoulders.*)

MADAME   (*stopping her*). No, thank you, it won't be
necessary, we shall be leaving very soon; we must get on
our way. It is important that we finish our journey as soon
as possible.

WIFE. I will see that Madame is not delayed.

MADAME. Oh, well—yes, thank you. (*Relinquishes her cloak and sits warming her hands again.* WIFE *exits up left, taking cloak with her.*) Marie (MARIE *is still up-stage busy with baggage.*), can you see anything through the window? Is anyone approaching?

MARIE (*peering through window*). It's as black as pitch, Madame.

MADAME. Open the door—look along the road.

> (MARIE *goes to door up right, opens it and peers into the darkness. Noise of storm increases.*)

MARIE (*closing door and coming back into room*). There is no one, Madame. That is . . . no stranger . . . just the coachman and the servant from the inn.

MADAME. Well, that's a comfort. Come and sit here and get warm . . . what a night! Why do storms come just when you have to get somewhere in a hurry?

> (MARIE *sits on stool below fireplace.* LANDLORD *and* GEORGES *enter up right carrying two smallish trunks of the period.*)

LANDLORD (*pointing up centre*). Here. (*They put baggage down up-stage.* LANDLORD *comes down to* MADAME.) The large black trunk, Madame?

MADAME (*turning to him*). Yes?

LANDLORD. Do you wish that brought in also?

MADAME. No, thank you. That won't be necessary; it is tightly strapped to the coach.

MARIE. But, Madame——

MADAME. It will be safe, Marie; in just a little while we shall be away again.

> (GEORGES *bows and exits down left.*)

LANDLORD (*with a broad smile*). Thank you, Madame. And now, you like some supper, yes?

MADAME. Please. As quickly as you can. And for the coachman you will arrange something?

LANDLORD. Certainly, Madame. (*To* MARIE.) And you, Miss, will you come?

MADAME (*interrupting*). Marie will have supper here —with me. Have you no other guests?

LANDLORD. Not tonight, Madame. The weather is too bad for travellers. And anyway, not many people pass through the village just now.

MADAME. And why not?

LANDLORD. The frontier is very closely watched, Madame, and there are not many more villages between us and the border.

MADAME. But what does that matter?

LANDLORD (*smiling broadly, and trying to pass it over lightly*). It matters very little, really—(*Shrugs*) you understand, in times like these, there are always rumours— Madame . . . and——

MADAME. What rumours?

LANDLORD (*confidentially*). Well, there have been arrests—so they say—traitors and royalists trying to escape to Switzerland—but don't let that worry you.

MADAME (*laughing*). Well, I am certainly not afraid of being arrested as a traitor . . . but anyway, we will continue our journey as soon as the horses are ready.

(YOUNG MAID *enters down left with tray, decanter, and two wine glasses. She stands just inside the door with them. The* LANDLORD *goes over and takes them.* MAID *exits down left.* LANDLORD *puts tray on serving-table left, and talks as he pours wine.*)

LANDLORD.   You would be wise to delay your departure until morning, Madame; the roads are very bad—almost impassable from the heavy rains.

MADAME.   Nevertheless, we must get on as soon as we can. It is impossible to delay any longer. I have a most important engagement. . . . Are you sure the roads are as bad as all that?

LANDLORD.   The mail-carrier said he had difficulty getting through the floods at the bridge even four hours ago. However (*he smiles genially*), supper will be ready soon, and then we can see. (*He brings over a glass of wine on the tray.*) Wine, Madame?

MADAME (*taking wine*). Thank you. (*She turns to* MARIE *who is still sitting down right.*) Wine, Marie?

MARIE.   Thank you, Madame.

LANDLORD.   Yes, Madame. (*He goes and pours a glass of wine and takes it to* MARIE.)

MARIE (*taking wine*). Thank you.

(LANDLORD *smiles, bows, and exits down left.*)

MADAME (*making sure she and* MARIE *are alone, and pacing up and down nervously as she talks*). Heaven help us, Marie. What a night! We'll never be there in time. Listen! (*She stands still. There is a sound of wind and rain outside.*) The storm seems worse than ever. . . . Listen! (*She is suddenly tense.*) Do you hear something?

(MADAME *goes a few steps up right towards door, then stands and listens.* MARIE *gets up and goes to her. They both stand listening.*)

MARIE (*moving away and peering through window, then*

coming down-stage). There is nothing, Madame. . . .(*She sits in the chair right of dining-table.*) I had better check and make sure I have a list of everything you need for tomorrow. (*She starts to rummage in a bag she picks up from among things on the window seat.*)

MADAME (*suddenly*). A horseman! Listen!

MARIE (*after listening a moment*). Madame, there is nothing, I assure you. Please don't upset yourself. I'm sure the gentleman was not really following us. He didn't look a bit like a thief.

MADAME. How can you tell? In these days thieves look like gentlemen, and gentlemen look like thieves. . . . One can't tell any more—besides, you heard what the landlord said. He might be a spy, Marie—and I hate spies . . . I——

MARIE. He was much too handsome to be a spy, Madame, or a thief. Besides, he wore his clothes too elegantly.

MADAME. Don't be silly, Marie, how could you tell? His cloak was all wet from rain—besides, it was too dark to see anything clearly. (*She sits on bench before the fire.*) Anyway, I didn't notice him particularly.

> (MADAME *looks into the fire.* MARIE *looks over at her and smiles a knowing smile.* MADAME *turns again.*)

All I know is that the last three times we halted at the coach station, he was there too. And the last time I pulled aside the coach curtains to look at the weather, I saw his black horse galloping just beside us. . . . I'm sure he is a highwayman . . . just waiting for an opportunity to rob us.

MARIE. He delayed rather a long time, Madame. It is some hours ago since we last saw him. . . . No . . . I think he is just a· gallant trying to work up a flirtation . . . and I'm sure he has not recognized you. . . . If he had, he would not dare—besides, not once did you lift your hood . . . that I remember.

MADAME. Well, Marie, in spite of what you say I am not convinced. (*Indignantly.*) Imagine any man being mad enough to try and carry on a flirtation with a woman when he has never seen her face. . . . I might be some terrible old hag from the Tuileries for all he knows . . . or I might be keeping my face covered because of the pox. No, even if he is no thief, I have not the slightest desire to indulge in any interchanges with a stranger . . . whoever he is . . . especially now when we are so short of time. . . . But—er —was he really so handsome, Marie?

MARIE. One of the handsomest men I have ever seen.

MADAME (*getting more and more interested*). Was he —er—dark or fair . . . or——(*She gets up and starts pacing the room again.*) Well, whoever he is, I am not the slightest bit interested. (*Angrily.*) If this delay goes on much longer, I shall be ruined. . . . Marie . . . look out again . . . is it still storming?

MARIE (*gets up quickly, goes to door, and peers out. Sound of wind and rain increases*). It sounds as bad as ever. (*Closes door and comes back and sits right of table again and finishes drinking her wine.*) The road is as black as pitch.

MADAME (*moving up and trying to peer through the window*). I think I can see a break in the clouds to the south . . . anyway, we can't be *very* far away from the frontier. (*She moves down left as she talks, and, pulling out a chair from the table, sits opposite* MARIE.) What time are we supposed to reach Aldkirch?

MARIE. About nine o'clock—but it is that now. . . .
I wish we could have gone on without this delay.

MADAME. So do I—but without fresh horses. . . . What
is this place we wait at?

MARIE. The Silver Crest Inn, Madame. I noticed the
sign as we got out of the coach.

MADAME. I mean the village. I have never travelled
this road before.

MARIE. I'm afraid I don't know, Madame. Shall I en-
quire? (*She starts towards door down left.*)

MADAME. No, never mind, it is of no consequence. We
shan't be here long. Come and sit down and get the cold
out of your bones.

(MARIE *sits on stool below fireplace.* LANDLORD
enters down left with wood for fire.)

LANDLORD. Supper will be served in a few minutes,
Madame.

MADAME. Thank you, then as soon as we've finished we
can continue our journey. Is the coachman having his supper? And have the horses been looked after?

LANDLORD. Yes, Madame.

MADAME. Then we shall soon be on our way, Marie.
Thank heaven!

LANDLORD. Tonight, Madame?

MADAME. Of course . . . why?

LANDLORD. It will be too difficult, Madame. The highway is in a shocking state. It is not safe; water is over the
bridges in many places—it may even be the road is washed
away. It will not be so bad in the morning. When it is
daylight you can see where you are going—but tonight
there is no moon.

MADAME (*anxiously*). Are you sure it is as bad as all that?

LANDLORD. In all truth, Madame. Travellers say it is one of the worst storms in living memory.

MADAME. What travellers? I thought you said there were scarcely any people on the road?

LANDLORD. Officers and soldiers, Madame, who tried to get through to Audicourt—they were in pursuit of some traitors trying to get through to the frontier. They left two hours ago, but already most of them are back. I have just spoken with some of them.

MADAME. Well, we shall see. It may change by the time we have had supper.

(*Landlord's* WIFE *enters down left.*)

LANDLORD. Wife, did Georges bring in the ladies' shawls and pillows from the coach?

WIFE. They are all in your room, Madame. The fires are lit, and the hot-water jugs filled. . . . I will show you the way.

(WIFE *exits up left, followed by* MADAME *and* MARIE. LANDLORD *crosses to down left.*)

LANDLORD (*calling from doorway*). Supper will be on the table in ten minutes.

(LANDLORD *exits, almost colliding with* YOUNG MAID *who is carrying a tray of cutlery and china for the table. She stands aside to let him pass, then puts tray on serving-table left. She starts setting places on the dining-table: for* MADAME *at top of table, for* MARIE *at stage left. She has placed knives and forks when she stops, looks at door down left, and listens at foot of stairs to make sure she is alone. Then she takes one of the lighted candles from the serving-table, goes quickly to the window, and describes two circles with the light so that they can be seen from outside. Then she runs and puts candle back in its place and goes on setting the table.*

In a moment, the door up right is pushed open very slowly and quietly, and a young GENDARME *pokes his head in and looks around.*)

GENDARME (*whispering*). Is the coast clear?

YOUNG MAID (*waving him back*). No. (*She shakes her head violently and waves him back. He backs away and closes the door quietly.*)

(*The* OLDER MAID *enters down left, bringing plates and soup bowls which she puts on serving-table.*

YOUNG MAID *gives an anxious glance up right to make sure* GASTON *is not in sight, then she starts to chatter as she works.*)

YOUNG MAID. Did you see the lady? I'll warrant she's some grand duchess or marchioness trying to reach the border. She's so beautiful, and her gown is so elegant.

OLDER MAID. You had better hold your tongue, my lass, or you'll be getting yourself into trouble. Duchesses are in bad odour hereabouts in these days. You'd better not let the gendarmes hear you talking such rubbish. (*Very snappishly.*) Besides, how should you know?

YOUNG MAID (*saucily*). Oh, I can tell.

OLDER MAID. How? I'd like to know. Are you a gendarme all of a sudden?

YOUNG MAID (*with a giggle*). No . . . but I took a good look at her when she was sitting by the fire and I brought the wine in. Her hair has signs of wig powder on it. (*As she talks she arranges chairs at the table for two.*)

OLDER MAID.   Oh, ho, ho . . . that's a good one.

YOUNG MAID.   Well, I thought I could tell—and besides Gaston told me.

OLDER MAID (*snappishly*).   And who, pray, is Gaston?

YOUNG MAID (*flustered*).   Did I say Gaston? . . . I meant Georges . . . you know . . .

OLDER MAID.   That old fool! What did he tell you?

YOUNG MAID.   Well, he told me she walked in a haughty sort of manner like aristocrats have. . . . It must be terrible to be a real aristocrat, I——

OLDER MAID.   Keep a quiet tongue in your head, silly. Before you know you'll be in trouble with the gendarmes. You have no call to be sorry for aristocrats—you know what the master said.

YOUNG MAID (*whispering mischievously*).   Well, anyway, I hope she gets away—so there—whoever she is——

OLDER MAID.   Ssh!

(*Landlord's* WIFE *enters down left with a large tureen of soup which she puts on serving-table.*)

WIFE (*to* YOUNG MAID).   Don't talk so much, girl. Your everlasting chatter—chatter—I could hear you away in the pantry. (*She looks over the table, then speaks to* OLDER MAID.) We shall need the large cruet from the serving-cupboard—and see if the hot bread is ready from the oven.

OLDER MAID.   Yes, Mistress. (*Exits down left.*)

WIFE (*calling after her*).   I expect they will need some more wine. Ask the master to bring up another bottle—and more glasses. I will advise Madame it is almost ready.

(WIFE *exits up stairs. Immediately she has disappeared, the* YOUNG MAID *rushes to the door up
right, opens it very cautiously, admitting* GASTON
*who tiptoes in, looking around to make sure no
one is about.* YOUNG MAID *runs to serving-table,
quickly ladles some soup into a bowl and brings
it to* GASTON. *He drinks greedily, and almost scalds
himself.* MAID *holds bowl while he controls his
spluttering, then he takes it and drinks more carefully. He finishes and wipes his mouth on his
sleeve, and grabs the* MAID *to kiss her. She pushes
him away towards door up right. He tiptoes out
and closes it quietly after him.*

Just as door is shut, MADAME *and* MARIE *appear
at top of the stairs up left.* YOUNG MAID *holds soup
bowl behind her back, and manages to get across
to the serving-table and put it back—although her
walk with her hands behind her back arouses*
MADAME'*s curiosity—but nothing is said.*)

MADAME   (*looks at table, very pleased, then sits at head,
and signals* MARIE *to sit at left*). How nice!
MARIE   (*sitting down*). Thank you, Madame.
      (LANDLORD *enters with covered food dishes which he
places on serving-table and gets ready to carve.*
      YOUNG MAID *stands below him ready to serve.*
OLDER MAID *enters with wine tray which she
puts on end of table. She places glasses beside*
MARIE *and has just reached* MADAME'*s left with
glass when there is a loud imperious knocking at
the door up right.*
      Everyone looks towards the door. LANDLORD
crosses and opens it admitting a pompous,

aggressive-looking man of middle age. He wears a heavy overcoat and a tricolour scarf across his shoulders. He looks quickly around the room, then approaches the table. YOUNG MAID, *terrified, disappears into kitchen.* OLDER MAID *remains by serving-table.* LANDLORD *closes the door and comes a few steps into room.*)

LANDLORD. Good evening, Mr. Mayor.

(*The man ignores the greeting. He crosses to within a few paces of* MADAME, *takes a document from his pocket, reads it to himself quickly, looks first at* MADAME, *then at* MARIE *as though he is comparing their appearance with whatever description is on the paper.*)

MAYOR (*speaking brusquely, almost rudely*). What is your name, Citizen?

MADAME (*resenting his tone and manner of staring— waiting a moment to gain her self-control. She speaks haughtily, half turning away from him*). First, sir, may I ask to whom I shall have the honour of giving my name, if I do so?

MAYOR (*importantly*). I am the Mayor of this village. Mayor Voulant.

MADAME (*with a slight inclination of her head*). I am Madame—er—Dupont. This is my maid, Marie.

MAYOR. You have papers—passports—yes?

MADAME. Why, yes—but of course—most certainly.

MAYOR (*holding out his hand*). Let me see them, Madame.

MADAME. I have not them on my person, sir. They are packed in my trunk.

MAYOR   (*to* MARIE). Yours?

MADAME.   Marie's papers are with mine—in the trunk.

MAYOR.   Nevertheless, I must see them.

MADAME.   Sir, you have no call to question us in this manner. We are citizens of France. We are not leaving the country.

MAYOR.   You are approaching a frontier town, Madame. Why would you be here travelling towards the border on a night like this?

MARIE   (*about to interrupt, but* MADAME *stops her with a gesture*). But, sir . . .

MADAME   (*haughtily*). We are on our own personal business, sir.

MAYOR   (*getting annoyed and almost shouting*). I demand your papers. In your trunk, you say. (*He looks around.*) Ah! (*He moves towards baggage on window seat.*)

MADAME.   Not that trunk, Mr. Mayor—let me see— Marie?

MARIE   (*nervously*). Yes, Madame?

MADAME.   Marie, in which trunk did we pack the papers? Do you remember?

MARIE.   The large black one, Madame.

MAYOR   (*looking about*). I don't see a large black trunk here.

MADAME.   It is still tied to the top of the coach, Mr. Mayor.

MAYOR.   And where is the coach?

MADAME.   It is in the mews while the horses are being rested.

MAYOR.   Well, it must be brought in. (*Turns to* LAND-LORD *who has been watching up right.*) *In here . . . at once.*

LANDLORD.   Yes, Mr. Mayor, I will see to it.

MADAME. It is quite heavy. May we have the help of your men?

MAYOR. Men?

MADAME (*with a glance towards up right*). The gentlemen who are waiting in the doorway—I am sure they are most anxious to assist.

MAYOR (*beckoning to* GASTON *and another* GENDARME *who have been lurking just outside the door*). Follow him.

> (*He points to* LANDLORD *who is waiting down left.*
> LANDLORD *and* GENDARMES *exit followed by* MAID.
> *The* MAYOR, *feeling very pleased with his importance, goes over and stands with his back to the fire.*)

MADAME (*looking very undisturbed and dignified, but friendly*). May I offer you a glass of wine while you are waiting, Mr. Mayor?

MAYOR (*beginning to weaken a little under the spell of her charm*). Er—er—thank you, Madame, I . . . (*Then he remembers his official dignity.*) No, no, thank you.

MADAME. It is very good wine—are you sure you can't be tempted?

MAYOR (*becoming suspicious that he is being teased*). No, thank you.

MADAME (*to* MARIE). A glass for me, please, Marie.

MARIE. Yes, Madame.

> (*She gets up, pours a glass of wine and hands it to*
> MADAME, *then goes and stands at the back of*
> MADAME's *chair.*)

MADAME. Thank you, Marie. (*Turns to* MAYOR.) Your good health, Citizen!

MAYOR (*feeling more uncomfortable every minute*). Thank you, Citizen. (*Speaking tersely.*) You say you are going to Audicourt?

MADAME. As you say, sir.

MAYOR. On personal business, you said?

MADAME (*bows assent*).

MAYOR. To visit members of your family, I presume?

MADAME (*brightly*). My uncle—he is the . . . the . . . the . . . town baker—no one in France can make brioche like those of my uncle—they are de-li-cious . . . I simply have to taste them again. I can hardly wait until we arrive.

MAYOR. Hmn! Hmn! I see.

> (*He is much relieved when the* GENDARMES *enter down left struggling with heavy trunk. They are followed by* LANDLORD *and his* WIFE *who stand to left of table, watching.*)

Ah! Here is the trunk. . . . Over here. . . . *Open it.*

> (GENDARMES *carry trunk to down right.*)

GASTON. Sir—it is locked—we have no keys.

MAYOR (*going to* MADAME *and holding out his hand*). Your key, Madame.

MADAME (*glancing over her shoulder*). Keys, Marie.

MARIE. Oh, yes, Mistress—I have them here.

> (*She fumbles in a large reticule that is hanging from her waist, brings out a large bunch of keys and hands them to* MADAME *who goes through them key by key, considering each with a puzzled expression and many shakes of the head, much to the* MAYOR's *annoyance. Suddenly she smiles most graciously at him.*)

MADAME. Ah, yes . . . this is the one . . . I knew it was somewhere here.

(*She detaches a key and hands it to him. He takes it, unlocks trunk, looks at top contents, then turns questioningly to* MADAME.)

(*Sweetly.*) The papers are in the bottom, sir.

(MAYOR *lifts a garment from trunk; it is obviously a very elaborate gown. He looks at it, then at* MADAME *whose expression betrays nothing. Then he walks over to the table and lays it down on the end opposite to that on which the meal is laid. He goes back to the trunk, lifts out several other costly-looking garments, and lays them on the table.* LANDLORD *and* WIFE *and* GENDARMES *watch in amazement, completely fascinated.* MAYOR *then lifts large jewel box from trunk and looks at* MADAME. *She gives no sign of any kind. He opens it, then, standing right of* MADAME, *lifts out a long string of pearls.*)

MAYOR. These are yours, Madame?

MADAME (*smiling sweetly*). Why, most certainly . . . to whom else could they belong?

MAYOR (*crossing and putting jewel box on table*). And these . . . these gowns?

MADAME. Why, of course . . . don't you like them? The papers are in the *bottom* of the trunk. It is a pity to give you so much trouble.

MAYOR (*furious*). Madame—enough of this nonsense! My suspicions are more than justified already. These gowns . . . these velvets . . . pearls . . . they alone prove you are no ordinary traveller.

(MARIE *makes a move up-stage.*)

Stop! Let no one move unless they have my permission.
You—(*He addresses the* GENDARMES.) outside and guard
that door. Let no one enter without advising me before-
hand. (GENDARMES *exit up right.*) And now, Madame, for
those papers.

> (*He returns to trunk, lifts up another gown, then
> stands a moment in amazement. Then from the
> trunk he lifts first a jewelled crown, and then a
> sceptre.* LANDLORD *and* WIFE *react in amazement.*)

Ah! Ah! Madame Dupont—so—you wear a crown. Rather
unusual, isn't it, for a baker's niece? (*He hands them to*
MARIE.) Here, place these with the other things on the table.

> (MARIE *takes them and puts them on the table, then
> moves up-stage again.*)

So—you were going to the frontier with the crown jewels
of France. . . . Your disguise is of no use, Madame Dupont.
. . . Now . . . without doubt, I know who you are.

MADAME   (*rising haughtily*). And who am I?

MAYOR.   You are Marie Antoinette—sometime Queen of
France. Can you deny that?

MADAME.   I deny nothing, Mr. Mayor . . . neither do
I affirm anything. I congratulate you on your skill at identi-
fication. (*She curtseys.*) Did you—er—expect the Queen
to pass this way on her flight to the border?

MAYOR   (*pompously*). Madame, France has no Queen.

> (*The* OLDER MAID *enters down left, stands inside the
> doorway gazing in amazement at the scene.*)

So—in the presence of these citizens (*With a wave of his
hand he indicates* LANDLORD, WIFE, *and* MAID.) I place you
under arrest.

MADAME. Without any further proof?

MAYOR (*pointing to robes, etc. on table*). Are these not proof enough? It is no wonder that you left this trunk outside instead of having it brought into the inn with the rest of your baggage. But I am not easily fooled—ah no— not by any means. (*He is puffed up with his own importance.*)

MADAME. Will you not at least examine my papers? They are in the bottom of the trunk.

MAYOR. What kind of a fool do you take me for? A borrowed passport I'll warrant—if there be one at all. . . . No. . . . Citizen Marie Antoinette—you can resign yourself to your fate. . . . I must get word to Paris immediately. . . . Protestations will avail you nothing. . . . As mayor I shall do my duty to my fellow-citizens.

MADAME (*with great dignity*). Sir . . . I have no desire to make protestations—no Queen would so demean herself.

MAYOR. Ah, ah, Madame . . . so you admit . . . (*Turns to* LANDLORD.) Mr. Innkeeper, no one is to leave or enter this room until I return. My men will be on guard outside —meantime (*sarcastically*), Your Majesty—I will go and make arrangements for your journey to Paris.

MADAME. Sir, I have no choice but to await your pleasure. . . . But will you please allow my maid and me to retire to our quarters?

MAYOR. Well, I see no objection to that.

MADAME. Come, Marie, and bring the large valise, please.

> (MADAME *and* MARIE *exit up stairs,* MARIE *carrying a large bag which she takes from among those on the window seat. The* MAYOR *goes to the door up right and beckons* GASTON *to come inside.*)

MAYOR (*to* GASTON). See no person enters or leaves by this door. I will send a man round to the rear.

> (GASTON *salutes.* MAYOR *exits up right.* LANDLORD *and* WIFE *exit down left. For a moment there is no one but* GASTON *on stage. The* YOUNG MAID *enters with a basket of hot rolls covered with a white napkin. She looks around surprised at the emptiness of the room, sees* GASTON, *barely suppresses a squeal of excitement, then, still carrying basket of rolls, runs over to him.*)

YOUNG MAID. Gaston! What are you doing here still?

GASTON. Hush! I'm on guard for the Mayor.

YOUNG MAID. What for? What are you guarding?

GASTON (*mysteriously*). You'll never guess.

YOUNG MAID. What? . . . Tell me.

GASTON. I can't.

YOUNG MAID. Why not, silly?

GASTON. It is very important—you promise you won't tell anybody else?

YOUNG MAID. Of course not—anyway, who could I tell? —I don't get out again until Sunday. (*Coaxing.*) Tell me—Gaston—please.

GASTON. See those things on the table?

YOUNG MAID (*turning. In her excitement at seeing* GASTON *she has not noticed them before. She starts to go towards table, but he pulls her back.*) Ooooh!

GASTON. Do you know who those belong to?

YOUNG MAID. The lady upstairs?

GASTON (*whispering*). Marie Antoinette.

YOUNG MAID (*smothering a little shriek*). Marie . . . you mean . . . the Queen. . . . (*Points to the stairs.*) She?

GASTON   (*nods*).

YOUNG MAID. Then you were right. You said she was
an aristocrat. . . . Here . . . quick . . . before the mistress
comes back.

> (*She lifts napkin, and offers him a roll from the
> basket.* GASTON *takes one but it is so hot that he
> almost drops it, before he finally succeeds in put-
> ting it in his pocket. Voices can be heard off right.*
> YOUNG MAID *rushes back to serving-table. There
> is an important knocking on the door.* GASTON
> *opens it and admits the* MAYOR *followed by some
> men citizens.*)

MAYOR. Enter—citizens.

> (*They come in and stand grouped right. The* MAYOR
> *comes down centre and faces them. The* LAND-
> LORD *and* WIFE *having heard knocking, enter down
> left. They stand by the serving-table.* WIFE
> *beckons* YOUNG MAID *to go back to the kitchen.*)

I have sent a messenger to the house of the Governor; he
should be here in a very short time. Meanwhile, my friends,
(*He rubs his hands together with pleasure.*) this is a very
important evening for us. Do you realize what it means?
We—citizens of France—hold as our prisoner the most
famous fugitive in the land—the Austrian who once dared
call herself Queen of France. . . . In a few days this village
will be a place to be famous in our history. You (*He makes
a grand gesture towards them.*) my fellow-citizens—your
names will live forever . . . and I . . . Mayor Voulant will
be the most noted personage in the land. (*He cackles.*) Ha!
Ha! What a piece of good fortune. (*He turns and points
to things on the table.*) See, my fellow patriots, what trophies
we have—a veritable king's—er—queen's ransom in jewels

—a fortune that, but for me, would have gone to a foreign country and been lost to France forever—and the royal robes. . . .

> (*As the men crowd round the table to see them, there is a sound of horses' hoofs and carriage wheels, and then an imperious rapping on the door. The citizens back away from the table. The* MAYOR *signals* GASTON *to open the door, and then stands centre. The* GOVERNOR *of the district and his* AIDE *enter.* GASTON *exits.*)

MAYOR (*loudly and importantly*). Welcome, gentlemen, welcome. Ah, what a night! I would not have disturbed you but for the importance of our news . . . Sir . . . I am detaining a prisoner——

GOVERNOR (*a very irritable and impatient old man*). Well, well, Mr. Mayor, surely that does not demand my presence? Have you brought me out on a night like this just to inform me that you have a prisoner? The garrison is here to give you what aid you need. You should have sent him to the guardhouse.

MAYOR. This is no ordinary prisoner, sir——

GOVERNOR. Oh! And why not, why not, pray? What's the matter with him? What d'you mean—no *ordinary* prisoner?

MAYOR. The prisoner is a lady, sir.

GOVERNOR (*after a moment's pause, and with a leer in his eye*). Oh, ho! What lady, may I ask?

MAYOR (*loudly, resenting the* GOVERNOR'*s flippancy*). Marie Antoinette!

GOVERNOR (*when he has recovered from his surprise; still slightly incredulous*). Do I—er—hear you aright—Mr. Mayor? You mean to say that Marie Antoinette is here—in this inn—now? Bah! What nonsense! She is not allowed to leave Paris. The woman you are detaining must be an impostor. What proof have you of her identity?

(MAYOR *steps aside and makes a grand gesture towards things on the table. The* GOVERNOR, *who is very near-sighted, peers at them.*)

MAYOR. What more evidence could we ask, sir, than these robes of state, these jewels? Here, before our eyes, the crown and sceptre of the woman who called herself the Queen of France.

GOVERNOR. Well—well—I am at a loss for the moment. This is indeed an unusual occasion . . . I . . .

(*One of the citizens comes forward. He has an aggressive tone and manner.*)

CITIZEN. Mr. Mayor—we—your fellow-citizens—commend you; and with the permission of our District Governor (*Bows to* GOVERNOR.) we propose that we form ourselves into a company of true patriots, and conduct this woman—this usurper—to Paris, and bring her before the National Tribunal.

MAYOR. Exactly what I was about to propose myself, fellow-citizens.

GOVERNOR (*irritably*). Certainly, certainly, gentlemen—er—citizens—all in good time; but we must act with discretion, meanwhile. By the way, Mr. Mayor, where is the lady in question—safely under guard, I hope?

MAYOR (*pointing upstairs*). In her bedchamber, sir.

ANOTHER CITIZEN (*coming forward*). Mr. Mayor, we do not doubt your word, of course, but the evidence of our own eyes as to the identity of the lady, would be even more conclusive. (*Turns.*) What do you say, citizens? (*They nod concurrence.*) Will you not ask the lady to appear before us so that we may assure ourselves?

MAYOR   (*turning to* LANDLORD *and his* WIFE *who are standing left.*) Ask Madame to come down immediately.

> (*Landlord's* WIFE, *very flustered, goes upstairs. Citizens continue to examine jewels, etc. Then* MADAME *appears at the top of the stairs. She has added jewels to her hair and dress, and is looking ravishingly beautiful. There is silence as the men gaze up at her.*)

MADAME.   Good evening, gentlemen. You desired my presence?

CITIZEN.   Just to convince ourselves, Madame.

> (*The* GOVERNOR *has just picked up an elaborate, jewelled gown.*)

MADAME   (*comes towards him and speaks with great charm and animation*). Ah! You have good taste, I see, sir.

> (*The* GOVERNOR, *who for the moment has lost sight of the seriousness of the occasion, recovers himself and throws robe back on table.*)

GOVERNOR.   Madame, you understand, of course, that we are fully aware of your true identity. I understand that you have not denied that you are—er—were the Queen. Our duty is to keep you here as our prisoner until the arrival of an escort from Paris.

MADAME.   Sir, I have denied nothing. At the moment, gentlemen, your word is law. . . . I await your pleasure.

> (*She turns and starts to go upstairs. Suddenly there is a great commotion outside: shouts and yells. Everyone turns to look towards the door up right.*)

MAYOR (*to* MADAME). Back to your room, at once.

(*One or two citizens move to guard foot of stairs after* MADAME *starts to go.* MARIE, *who has entered on landing up left, calls.*)

MARIE (*frightened*). Oh, Madame, please come away.

(MADAME *remains on landing watching.* MARIE *remains with her. The door up right is flung open and a* GENDARME *rushes in. He is agitated and breathless.*)

GENDARME. Mr. Mayor—Mr. Mayor—we have captured Polignac—or Lambelle . . .

GOVERNOR (*stepping forward*). Who? What's that you say?

GENDARME. He was riding like the wind, sir, to the frontier. We had quite a task to catch him—then he tried to escape from us—fought like a devil.

GOVERNOR. Well, well, man—who is he—who is he—and where?

GENDARME. He tried to pretend he was just an innocent traveller, but one of the gendarmes recognized him. He'd seen him in Paris.

GOVERNOR. Bring him in here at once.

(GENDARME *salutes and goes out, returning almost immediately with a handsome young man followed by a second* GENDARME *with fixed bayonet. The young man's clothes are rich, but they are muddy and bedraggled; he has lost his hat and his cloak is torn.*)

What is your name, young man?

ANTON. Anton Lefevre, sir.

GOVERNOR.   Why did you ride away when the gendarmes approached you?

ANTON.   I am in a great hurry.

GOVERNOR.   Why? Where are you going—in this time— and in this weather?

ANTON.   Aldkirch, sir.

GOVERNOR.   So? And what business have you there?

ANTON.   Just—personal business—sir.

MARIE   (*who is on landing exclaims softly, but not softly enough; the* MAYOR *looks up at her enquiringly, but her face betrays nothing. Then she whispers to* MADAME.) Madame —it is the young man who——

MADAME.   Sssh!

GOVERNOR   (*to* MAYOR). Let me see his papers.

MAYOR   (*to* ANTON). Your papers?

ANTON   (*searching in torn pocket of his cloak*). I . . . I . . . have them no longer, sir. They must have fallen in the mud when the gendarme pulled me from my horse.

MAYOR.   So—a most strange coincidence—another traveller in a hurry to reach the frontier—and with no papers to prove his identity.

ANTON.   I am bound for the frontier, sir, only as far as . . .

(*He catches sight of the robes and jewels on the table and moves towards them. The* GOVERNOR *by this time is a bit weary, and sits in the chair right of table, taking snuff, and watching what is going on.*)

MAYOR.   You seem surprised. Perhaps you—er—recognize these?

(ANTON *moves to up-stage end of table, and is about to pick up sceptre, when a* GENDARME *pulls him back roughly. He looks over to the trunk down right, and then back to the things on the table, and then suddenly bursts out laughing. The* GENDARME *tightens his grip and pulls* ANTON *away right. The* GOVERNOR *turns and beckons* GENDARME *to bring* ANTON *to him.*)

GOVERNOR. Your laughter, my young buck, will be of short duration. There is nothing amusing to me in an attempt to smuggle crown jewels across the border, and take them from their rightful owners—the citizens of France.

ANTON (*in mock seriousness*). My apologies, gentlemen. I had not realized the seriousness of the situation.

GOVERNOR (*getting up very angry, and turning to* MADAME *who has been watching the scene from the top of the stairs*). There is no doubt, Madame, that this man is one of your accomplices.

MADAME (*haughtily*). This gentleman is a stranger to us.

(ANTON *for the first time becomes aware of* MADAME. *As she slowly descends the stairs, he stands watching her in admiration.*)

GOVERNOR. A likely story.

MAYOR. Then why did your maid remark, "It is the young man . . ."? I heard her.

MADAME. That is soon explained. This man followed our coach as we journeyed from Paris. At least I believe this was the man. He is a stranger to us, though, so I cannot be sure. Through the storm and blackness I did not see his face too clearly; as a matter of fact, gentlemen, I might even recognize his horse the better. Anyway, who is he—a highway robber?

GOVERNOR (*getting more and more peevish*). Let's stop all this nonsense. A man does not follow the coach of the Queen—er—ex-Queen of France in ignorance of the occupant's identity at a time like this—and near the frontier, too. I——

MADAME (*interrupting*). I must still affirm, sir, I have never known this gentleman in my life.

(ANTON *has been looking at* MADAME *intently as she talks.*)

ANTON. The Queen of France! Marie Antoinette! Travelling to Aldkirch tonight!

MADAME. So these gentlemen claim.

MAYOR. I'll wager it is no news to you, sir.

ANTON (*goes down on his knees before* MADAME, *and raises her hand to his lips, then stands and bows low before her*). Your Majesty—I crave your pardon. Had I but suspected it was a queen whom I presumed to follow, I would have died rather than forget the respect due so noble a lady. Now I am aware of my presumption, I crave your pardon for——

GOVERNOR (*very angry*). Come, come, enough of this. Do you realize you are our prisoners?

MADAME (*to* ANTON). My pardon I grant most willingly.

MAYOR (*breaking in between them*). That is enough. We'll soon show how much your pardon amounts to, Madame. We know how to deal with traitors and royalists. (*To* GENDARMES.) This man is under arrest, remember. (GENDARMES *take him by the arms and pull him right.*)

GOVERNOR (*feeling he should take charge of the situation here*). In spite of this man's eloquence and devotion, Madame, and also your denial as to having known him previously, it is obvious that he is no stranger; he may even be a member of your court. This will come out in time, but, for the present, he will remain under arrest until the escort arrives for all three of you. In the meantime, you and your maid will retire to your own apartment upstairs.

> (ANTON, *standing between* GENDARMES, *bows deeply as* MADAME *turns away and walks slowly upstairs towards* MARIE *who is still standing at the top. As she turns, she smiles at* ANTON. *The* GOVERNOR *signals the landlord's* WIFE *to follow* MADAME *upstairs; he then turns and is about to give orders to the* GENDARMES *concerning* ANTON, *when there is the sound of a coach stopping outside, and then a knock on the door up right.* GENDARMES *tighten their hold on* ANTON. MAYOR *looks questioningly at* GOVERNOR, *who nods. The* MAYOR *opens the door. Two well dressed men enter. One is middle-aged, plump, jolly-looking, and rather overdressed. The other, his secretary, is more sedate and younger.*)

TRAVELLER   (*enters and looks rather surprised at the number of people standing watching him. He is facing left and does not notice* ANTON *and the* GENDARMES *who are down right*). Is the innkeeper here?

LANDLORD.   Yes, sir. I am he, sir.

TRAVELLER.   Can you get us supper quickly? We are in a hurry to—— (*He becomes aware that everyone is watching him intently.*) Anything amiss, gentlemen? Has there been a robbery?

MAYOR   (*coming round to left of* TRAVELLER). Excuse me, gentlemen. I am Mayor Voulant. May I see your passports, please?

TRAVELLER (*genially*). Certainly, certainly, my friend, though we shan't need them. We're not crossing the border, just going as far as Aldkirch.

A CITIZEN. Oh, ho! Another one bound for Aldkirch.

MAYOR (*pompously*). Nevertheless, gentlemen, I must ask for your papers.

TRAVELLER (*a bit surprised at the* MAYOR's *tone*). By all means. (*Turns to his secretary who stands behind him left.*) Give them to him, Gustave. (*To* MAYOR.) My secretary has them.

> (*While the* SECRETARY *is getting papers from a leather satchel he carries, the* TRAVELLER *crosses down left to talk to* LANDLORD *who is standing by the serving-table.* TRAVELLER *stands with his back to room, discussing requirements for supper.* MAYOR *reads the papers and hands them to* GOVERNOR *who has sat down again.* GOVERNOR *looks them over and returns them to* SECRETARY.)

GOVERNOR. Everything seems to be in order, gentlemen. We need not detain you further from your supper.

LANDLORD (*going to door left*). The smoking-room is this way, sir.

> (*The* TRAVELLER *turns as the* GOVERNOR *speaks and then sees* ANTON *and the* GENDARMES *down right.*)

TRAVELLER (*in amazement*). Why! What the . . . Anton! What's happened to you? In the name of the Saints.

ANTON. I am under arrest, sir.

TRAVELLER. Under arrest?

GOVERNOR (*suspiciously*). This man is a friend of yours?

TRAVELLER. A friend! (*He bursts out laughing.*) He's my brother's son. He should have been in Aldkirch hours ago. What's he been up to? Some woman's bright eyes, I bet, are responsible. (*He then notices the half-empty trunk and the things on the table.*) How did this get here and——

MAYOR. You recognize this trunk and these garments, sir?

TRAVELLER (*to* ANTON). Is this some of your doing?

ANTON. Uncle, I swear that until I came here tonight —or rather was *brought* here—I have not seen this trunk or those things (*Points to table.*) since two years ago in . . .

GOVERNOR (*pettishly*). What *is* all this nonsense? (*To* TRAVELLER.) This man—whoever he is—whom you claim to be your brother's son, is under arrest as an enemy of the Republic.

TRAVELLER. Anton? . . . In the name of Heaven——

MAYOR. This man is a traitor, sir. Caught red-handed.

TRAVELLER. Traitor—rubbish—I——

GOVERNOR (*interrupting*). I regret to tell you, sir, that this young man—be he your nephew or not—was travelling as an escort for Marie Antoinette—one-time Queen of France.

MAYOR. They were endeavouring to escape to the frontier, but the storm delayed the ladies, and the—the attention of the gendarmes interrupted the gentleman, and upset their plans.

TRAVELLER. Marie Antoinette! With Anton! (*Turns to* ANTON.) Come, my boy, what sort of jest is this? Don't carry things too far.

ANTON. I can assure you, Uncle, the jest, if any, is none of my making.

MAYOR.   It is no jest, sir. The woman, too, is here under arrest while we wait the escort from Paris. This young man will be returned with her to face the proper authorities.

TRAVELLER   (*to* GOVERNOR). Pardon me, sir, I am not very clear what this is all about, but this young man is my nephew. I have known him since he was an infant. Besides, he has only just arrived back in France after being two years in England at the . . .

GOVERNOR   (*shaking his head*). He will have to convince the proper authorities.

TRAVELLER   (*growing angry, turns to* ANTON). Speak up. What foolishness have you been guilty of? (*To* GOVERNOR.) He has never even seen Marie Antoinette—let alone travel with her.

ANTON.   Sir, at the risk of your displeasure, I must confess the gentlemen are right. I have placed my life at the service of a Queen who is the loveliest woman I have ever set eyes on.

TRAVELLER   (*puzzled*). Anton! Have you gone mad? What is——

MARIE.   Your pardon, Mr. Mayor. (*Everyone turns to look at her.*)

MAYOR.   Well, what is it?

MARIE.   My Mistress would like to speak with you.

MAYOR.   Tell your Mistress I can have no conversation with her in private. If she cares to come down here where we have witnesses . . .

MARIE.   But it is of great importance, sir.

MAYOR.   Tell your Mistress to come here.

   (MADAME *steps forward to top of stairs.*)

MADAME.   Here I am, sir.

(*Everyone in the room turns to look at her as she stands for a moment, then the* TRAVELLER *bursts into roars of laughter. After a moment she joins in.* ANTON *is looking at her with admiration. Everyone else looks bewildered.*)

GOVERNOR   (*furious*).   What is this unseemly conduct? Has everyone gone mad?

TRAVELLER.   A thousand pardons, sir, but this is, to say the least, an unusually amusing circumstance. (*He controls his mirth with difficulty.*)

MAYOR.   There is nothing amusing in the arrest of traitors, especially when one of them is the greatest enemy of France —an Austrian usurper who——

TRAVELLER   (*ignoring the* MAYOR's *outburst, crosses to the foot of the stairs and holds out his hand to* MADAME). Your Majesty, please descend.

(MADAME *walks slowly down with great dignity. The* TRAVELLER *leads her centre.*)

Gentlemen, allow me to introduce you. This lady has been the Queen of many countries—and of many hearts—but she has never laid claim to the throne of France. Allow me to introduce Mademoiselle Sidonie of the Theatre Royale.

MAYOR   (*in dismay*).   An actress!

TRAVELLER.   The greatest in France. The leading lady of my company. And here (*He turns and holds out his other hand to* ANTON.) Anton Lefevre, my favourite nephew, just back from two years at the famous Drury Lane Theatre in London, England. We are on our way to play a two-weeks engagement in Aldkirch.

MAYOR   (*very angry*).   So, Madame, you have been playing tricks on us?

GOVERNOR   (*looking at* MADAME *with a bit of a leer*).
Well, well, this is *most* unethical.

MAYOR. Unethical!! Unethical!! It's . . . It's . . .
(*He can't find words for his rage.*)

MADAME. Forgive me, sir. But it was really your own
fault. Had you read my passport—and it is in the bottom
of my trunk—I would not have had an opportunity to star
in such a tempting role (*Turns to* GOVERNOR.) and before
such a distinguished audience.

GOVERNOR   (*begins to weaken, and is just about to speak
when . . .*)

MAYOR   (*dramatically*). Hold! Gentlemen. Don't let us
be fooled too easily. There is some evidence we have forgotten; evidence that proves all these stories are just—just
a pack of lies.

> (*All turn towards him as he points dramatically to
> the jewels, etc. on the table.*)

Have you forgotten those—the crown jewels of France?

> (MADAME *goes to table, takes crown and places it on
> her head, then, holding the sceptre in her hand, she
> comes down centre.*)

TRAVELLER   (*coming forward beside her and bowing*).
Gentlemen, the Queen of Sidonia requests your presence as
her guests in the stage box of the Grande Theatre at Aldkirch tomorrow night.

> (MADAME *curtseys;* ANTON *bows as*
>
> CURTAIN FALLS.)

THE PIGEON WITH THE SILVER FOOT

A LEGEND OF VENICE

by

PAMELA HANSFORD JOHNSON

and

C. P. · SNOW

CHARACTERS

Of to-day

Mary
Joanna
The Waiter at Florian's

Of yesterday

Bianca
Mario
The Customer
The Beggar
The Lover

THE PIGEON WITH THE SILVER FOOT

SCENE: *The Piazzo San Marco, in Venice. In front and to one side a few yellow tables and chairs, representing Florian's cafe.*

The time is near-midnight in late October. Two girls, MARY *and* JOANNA, *just out of their teens, are sitting over their ice-creams outside Florian's. The* WAITER *is fidgeting in the background.* MARY *is whistling softly to herself.*

JOANNA. What's that you're whistling?

MARY. Whistling? Oh . . . I think it was something I heard this morning. One of the gondoliers was humming it.

JOANNA. It's pretty. I wonder what the words are?

MARY. Do you think it's a song?

JOANNA. Oh, of course. You can almost hear the words that go with it. I wish I could hear them.

(MARY *goes on whistling, very softly and sweetly.*)

I am glad we decided to make it Venice!

MARY. So am I. I think it must be more beautiful now, in late autumn, even if there aren't so many people about.

JOANNA. It was an awful business saving up, wasn't it?

MARY. But worth it.

JOANNA. We shall be as poor as church mice for the rest of the year.

MARY. I don't care. You know, I shall never forget this: sitting outside Florian's, where Lord Byron used to sit, looking at the moon shining on Saint Mark's.

JOANNA. We could do with a Byron, I suppose. Perhaps one ought to have a romance in Venice. There's something missing, really, for two girls travelling alone.

(*The* WAITER *listens, smiling, to this exchange.*)

MARY. We are young. There's plenty of time for us.

JOANNA. Sometimes I think we're just superfluous women.

MARY. Oh, come! Neither of us is twenty-two yet!

JOANNA. Not quite. Nearly.

MARY. There was such a handsome young man in the Piazza this morning, when I was feeding the pigeons. It's fun feeding the pigeons, isn't it? You can feel their hearts beating against your wrist. . . . Yes, he was handsome. Did you notice him?

JOANNA. Not particularly.

MARY. Wouldn't it be wonderful if we met some foreign prince——

JOANNA. Two princes.

MARY. All right. Met two foreign princes, and they fell in love with us——

JOANNA. We'll have to make do with what we can get. And working girls don't marry princes. That's a story. It never was true and it never will be.

(*The midnight bell begins to chime.*)

MARY. Oh, I say, it is getting late! *Cameriere!*

WAITER. *Si, Signorina.*

MARY   (*her Italian is very limited*). *Voglio la-er* . . .
la conta . . . prego.

WAITER   (*in good brisk English*). Here you are, miss.
All ready.

MARY.   Oh, thank you!—Do you speak English?

WAITER.   Pretty well. Yes. I have lived in England.

MARY.   I'm afraid we've kept you too late. You're wanting to close down.

WAITER.   Oh . . . In the season it is all hours. But now,
the nights grow cold. There was snow in Padova yesterday.

JOANNA.   *We* haven't felt cold!

WAITER.   The magic keeps the cold out, yes? (*To*
MARY) The Signorina was whistling a very old song just
now.

MARY.   Oh! Do you know it?

WAITER.   Everyone knows the tune. But not many know
the words.

JOANNA.   Do you know them?

WAITER.   Oh, yes. *Certamente.*

JOANNA.   Sing them for us!

WAITER.   Ah! You think because the Italians sing, *all*
Italians sing. Many have voices like frogs. I have a voice
like a frog. But this I will tell you: the song belongs to the
legend.

MARY.   What legend is that?

WAITER.   The legend of the pigeon with the silver foot.
It is a very old one. You were talking just now of princes
who come to marry poor young ladies with no money——

JOANNA.   It was only fun.

WAITER.   There was once upon a time a very poor young
lady called Bianca, a lacemaker, who lived behind the
church of San Cassian. Now this young lady longed for a
handsome lover——

(*The light fades and leaves the stage in darkness.*
BIANCA'*s voice is heard singing. After the first
verse of the song, the middle arch, representing her
home, is brightly illuminated.* BIANCA, *a girl of
sixteen, is examining the lace she has made during
the day, and is singing rather sadly to herself. The
tune of her song is the one* MARY *has been whistling. Her costume is roughly that of the mid-
eighteenth century, but very poor and ragged.*

*Her room is bare but for a bed, a chair, and a
small table, but on the last is a cheap but pretty
cup of Venetian glass.*)

BIANCA (*sings*).
Moon and waves of the white lagoon
 Are bringing my love to land,
And the stars fade as my love flashes
 The ring on his milk-white hand.
Serene he steps from the sill of the dawn,
 And the smile that he saves for me
Catches his eyes, as St. Mark's catches
 The sun across the sea.

(MARIO, *a young man, enters and walks along arches
and knocks at* BIANCA'*s door.*)

MARIO. Bianca!

BIANCA. Mario! How late you are! I was just going
to bed.

MARIO. Aren't you pleased to see me?

BIANCA. Oh, yes, of course, but . . .

MARIO (*stepping into the room and sitting down on
bed*). But what?

BIANCA. I'm so tired! So tired!

MARIO. *Poveretta!*

BIANCA.   It's been such a long, hard day. And all the days are the same.

MARIO.   I know. You work too hard.

BIANCA.   And my eyes are so sore from making the lace. You can't think how sore they are and how tired I am. But I mustn't be selfish. Life is hard for us all, and your hands are blistered from the oars.

MARIO.   My hands are healed again when I put them on your shoulders.

BIANCA.   Let me go please. I know what you've come to say. You say it every night.

MARIO.   And I know what you say, too; but I shall never stop asking. Let us be married, Bianca, darling, and we can at least be poor and tired together, but have the fun of laughing together a little as well.

BIANCA.   I can't, dear. We've been brought up side by side since we were children. We know each other too well. And besides——

MARIO.   Besides, what?

BIANCA.   You think I am silly.

MARIO.   I could think you were the silliest girl in the world and love you just the same.

BIANCA.   Well, then—I have a very queer feeling that my love is waiting for me. That he is very handsome and proud and rich, and that one day he will come and make me a lady.

MARIO.   And what shall I do if he does?

BIANCA.   You will marry Caterina, Bertolo's daughter. I have seen you look at her. You would make love to Caterina if you weren't so sorry for me. If you didn't feel bound to me.

MARIO.   What rubbish! I never looked at anyone but you.

BIANCA.   I have seen you look sideways into Caterina's black eyes.

MARIO.   They're not black. They're blue.

BIANCA.   And you tell me you have never looked at Caterina!

MARIO.   Oh! You're a terrible girl! You don't deserve a fellow like me. (*Trying to embrace her. Tenderly teasing her.*) Do you now? Tell me?

BIANCA.   Neither of us deserves to have to marry the other simply because everyone says we ought to.

MARIO.   Everyone expects it. And they all say: "Two can live as cheaply as one."

BIANCA.   I don't want to live cheaply any more. I'm so tired of working that sometimes, when I get up in the morning and look at my lace, I wish it would turn to foam and that I was under the foam, just sleeping, and sleeping forever and ever.

MARIO.   Oh, my pet! You mustn't say that.

BIANCA.   How can I help it? It's so hard, when you're not very old, to do nothing but work and sleep even to get a loaf of bread. Sometimes I earn so little that I'm afraid I shall have to sell my beautiful cup.

MARIO.   You love it, don't you?

BIANCA.   It was the only present my mother gave me. And, of course, it's not worth very much, but it's pretty! Isn't it?

MARIO.   Very pretty.

BIANCA.   My grandfather was a glass-blower. He was poor, too, as we've always been, and had to sell everything he made except just this one thing, which he kept for himself. I always feel that so long as I have it I shall somehow be all right. But sometimes I'm frightened that even that

will have to go—and then—I think I should die. (*Pause.*)
And sometimes I feel I shouldn't be sorry if I did. It would
only be like going to sleep and not having to get up in the
morning.

MARIO. Don't, my darling! You're only a child.

BIANCA. We are both lost children, both of us, and
nobody cares about us, and nobody ever will, unless——

MARIO. Unless what?

BIANCA. I am right about my lover.

MARIO. Your handsome, rich, proud lover. Am I nothing
at all to you?

BIANCA. If you would stop thinking about me you could
marry Caterina Bertolo, whom you love, and Caterina's
father would give you work in his boat-house, and you
wouldn't be poor any more.

MARIO. Oh, be quiet about Caterina!

BIANCA. She doesn't interest you at all?

MARIO. Not at all.

BIANCA. She has a lovely voice, and sings very high.

MARIO. Very low.

BIANCA. She has little feet.

MARIO. Not so little as yours.

BIANCA. But pretty?

MARIO. Pretty-ish.

BIANCA. In her red shoes with the stars on the toes.

MARIO. They came from Florence, those shoes!

BIANCA (*laughs*). Oh, oh, oh!

MARIO. Why are you laughing?

BIANCA. Because you are so uninterested in Caterina
Bertolo! Dear Mario, you must go now, because I am very,
very tired and if I don't go to bed now I shall sleep till noon.

MARIO. I shall come again tomorrow night and say all
the same things.

BIANCA. No, dear: it's no use.

> (*She goes to the door to bid him good-bye but at that moment a masked and cloaked lady,* THE CUSTOMER, *comes swiftly along the arches. She is attended by two torch-bearers who take up their positions at either side of the arch.*)

CUSTOMER. Is this the home of Bianca the lace-maker by the church of San Cassian?

> (MARIO *steps back into room.* BIANCA *remains on doorstep.*)

BIANCA. *Gentilissima signora,* if you will please step in——

CUSTOMER. It will please me better if you will step out, and a little way out of earshot of this young man. The night is warm and I should stifle in your small room.

BIANCA. My room is small but clean, and the windows are open to the water——

CUSTOMER. If you please.

> (*She draws* BIANCA *out, leaving* MARIO *listening.*)

Now *signorina,* I have a fancy to buy your lace. A handkerchief, only a handkerchief——

BIANCA. But I must fetch my lace to show you!

CUSTOMER. How shall I know better than you what is good and what is bad? You shall sell me the most beautiful handkerchief you have, with the linen no more than an inch square, and the lace a hand's breadth deep all round: and you shall not sell it for money.

BIANCA. *Signora,* it is by money that I live. I would like to give you a handkerchief, because it would be foolish of me to pretend that you are not the most grand, and I am sure, the most beautiful customer I ever had, but if you give me no money I shall have no breakfast.

CUSTOMER. Young man, fetch the girl a handkerchief, the finest of all.

BIANCA. But he doesn't know where to look! He doesn't understand at all about lace. He doesn't know the difference between Venetian point and a fishnet——

CUSTOMER. The first his hand lights upon will be the finest. You shall see.

(MARIO *comes out with a handkerchief which he gives to* BIANCA.)

MARIO. Will this do? This was the first I saw.

(BIANCA *looks at it. Stares dumbfounded at him.*)

Isn't it all right?

CUSTOMER (*taking the handkerchief*). (*To* BIANCA) You see? It is as I said. (*To* MARIO) You are an amiable young man and I like your face, but you had better go home now. You have played your part and shall have your reward.

MARIO. But I don't understand——

BIANCA. Do as she says, Mario.

MARIO. I—oh, very well. *A rivederla,* Bianca. I shall see you tomorrow. (*Exit.*)

CUSTOMER. He will not see you tomorrow because at midnight you will be feeding the pigeons in the Square of Saint Mark's.

BIANCA. But there are no pigeons in the square at midnight! They are all roosting in the spires and roof tops with their heads under their wings.

CUSTOMER. We shall see. (*She is putting the handkerchief away in her sleeve.*)

BIANCA. *Signora,* that will be one ducat——

CUSTOMER. I told you. I do not buy with money.

BIANCA. Then with what?

CUSTOMER. With a handsome, rich, proud lover.

BIANCA. Oh, you must have heard what I said to Mario! You must have been listening! I know—you were in your gondola beneath my window and you listened to it all!

CUSTOMER. My good girl, do I seem to you like a listener at casements or keyholes? Really, I shall be out of patience with you.

BIANCA. Then how——

CUSTOMER. Be quiet and don't ask questions. If you want your lover, you will do as I say. At the end of every day you will buy a *schei*'s worth of grain. Every night at twelve you will go to Saint Mark's Square and feed the pigeons. Many will come to you, but you must watch for the pigeon with the silver foot. And when the silver pigeon alights upon your hands, clinging to your fingers and pecking grain from your palm, your lover will come to you from the lagoon and make you his bride.

BIANCA. But I have no money for grain! I can hardly feed myself.

CUSTOMER. You have a little money saved for a rainy day and you shall spend it. Every night you shall go to the Square until the pigeons fly to you but if one single night you fail—your lover will never come, and you will live in this hovel for the rest of your life.

BIANCA. But *signora*, how shall I believe all this?

CUSTOMER. Did you believe Mario would bring me the right handkerchief? To your bed now, and tomorrow, do as I say. (*She turns to go, turns back.*) There is nothing else you have to sell?

BIANCA. I have a great deal of lace——

CUSTOMER. Not lace. Something hard and bright that glitters on your table.

BIANCA (*stiffening*). That is not for sale.

CUSTOMER. Not for money?

BIANCA. Nor for a lover.

CUSTOMER. Are you sure?—We shall see. Tomorrow in the Piazza at midnight. (*To torch-bearers.*) Come!

(*She sweeps off and the light goes out. The* WAITER'S *voice is heard in the darkness.*)

WAITER. Now Bianca did not know what to believe or not to believe, but the more she thought about her strange customer the more she was tempted to do as the lady said, and see what would happen. So on the next evening she bought a little grain out of her tiny store of money so carefully hoarded, and set out for St. Mark's Square.

(*As he continues to talk, the light falls to the side of the stage, and the scenes he describes are mimed by* BIANCA.)

She stood in the cool night with her palm outstretched, looking upwards towards the domes of St. Mark's, that glistened in the moonbeams as if they were spread with fine snow. There was a smile on her face, a little unbelieving, a little bitter, perhaps, because she was afraid a joke was being played on her. But then the first pigeon flew down and clung to her fingers. She gave a cry of delight, and stroked its wings as it pecked away at the grain. She touched its little feet, but they were rosy-red in the moonbeams, not silver at all. And then the birds came flying from everywhere, beating about her shoulders, cooing against her cheeks. They flew upon each other's backs, struggling for a place upon her fingers, on her palm or her wrist or her arm, and she could not help laughing for sheer surprise, and because it was so funny to see them fight. With her free hand she pushed them apart, searching among beaks and feathers for the silver foot, but there was no silver foot. And as suddenly as the birds had come they flew away, and all the grain was gone, and Bianca, with her hands empty at her sides, so very disappointed and sad, went slowly on her way back to her home behind the church of San Cassian.

JOANNA'S VOICE.   Oh, poor old Bianca! I feel so sorry for her.

MARY'S VOICE.   But it came out all right in the end, didn't it? I mean, she had a lover, only she didn't realize it, and——

WAITER.   *Zitto, signorina!* You run too fast. You shall hear what happened if you will be patient a little while longer. Next night the same thing happened, and again the next, and again and again, until——

      (*The light goes up in the centre arch.* BIANCA *is sitting on the edge of her bed in tears.* MARIO *is sitting helpless at her side.*)

BIANCA.   All my money has gone! I can't buy any more grain, not a single lentil. I can't even buy supper for myself.

MARIO.   I wish I hadn't eaten mine. Not that it was much.

BIANCA.   What was it?

MARIO.   Only a bit of bread.

BIANCA.   With a sausage?

MARIO.   Well, only a little piece.

BIANCA.   And wine? Did you have wine?

MARIO.   Only a glass of wine. And the cheapest wine, too. You wouldn't have liked it, it was so sour.

BIANCA.   I would have liked anything, *anything*!

MARIO.   Oh, I am so sorry! The thought of my own supper

chokes me. But you know, you'd have eaten, too, if only it hadn't been for those wretched pigeons!

BIANCA. Don't say that! Don't you see what a miracle it was that they came at all?

MARIO. I expect you'd come running pretty quickly if anyone suddenly offered you a meal at midnight. Nothing wonderful about that.

BIANCA. Oh, I'm sure it's wonderful! You should have seen them. They came down in a great whirling cloud, and their feathers were all pink and green in the moonlight, like the glass my grandfather used to blow, and they came around my feet till I was paddling in a sea of pigeons!

MARIO. But they were just ordinary birds. None of your silver-footed sort. What a lot of nonsense you believe!

BIANCA. You're hateful, Mario! And you can go home. I don't want you here.

MARIO. Don't be so silly.

BIANCA. I mean it. Go home! Go home, do you hear? As if it isn't bad enough to be cheated and hungry, without being laughed at into the bargain!

MARIO. So you admit you were cheated?

BIANCA. Go away.

MARIO. If I go, I shan't come back.

BIANCA. Don't, then, don't! Go to Caterina Bertolo and talk your good, sound common sense to her! She'll like it better than I do. (*With dignity, showing him the door.*) *A rivederla*, Mario.

MARIO (*after a pause*). *Addio*. (*He makes her a sweeping mock bow and goes out into the darkness.*)

> (BIANCA *flings herself at full length on the bed, weeping, and kicking her heels. She is in a small tantrum of disappointment, and she is, indeed,*

dreadfully hungry. The CUSTOMER *appears rather suddenly in the doorway.*)

CUSTOMER.   It is half-past eleven by the parish bell and you have not set out for San Marco.

BIANCA.   You again! Oh, I don't want to be rude, *signora*, anyone will tell you I am never rude, but I wish I had never set eyes on you!

CUSTOMER.   Rudeness doesn't bother me. Why have you not set out for San Marco?

BIANCA.   Because I have no grain left.

CUSTOMER.   Then buy some.

BIANCA.   I can't. I have no more money. I haven't even enough to buy myself supper!

CUSTOMER (*impatiently, stepping into house*).   Oh, you're a silly girl! You don't deserve a lover.

BIANCA.   Why am I silly? Why should you call me silly because I have no money left? Money is easy for ladies like you.

CUSTOMER.   You could find money.

BIANCA.   How?

CUSTOMER.   You have still something left to sell.

BIANCA.   If the *signora* would care to look at the veil I finished today, the finest net, so fine it would only be a shadow over her golden hair, trimmed with the most delicate *point de Burano*——

CUSTOMER.   I do not want any lace. In my house I have coffer upon coffer of lace far finer than yours, all laid down in lavender. I will buy this. (*She takes up the cup.*)

BIANCA.   That is not for sale! Not for a thousand ducats, *signora*!

CUSTOMER.   I am not offering you a thousand ducats. I am offering you the price of one packet of grain.

BIANCA. I don't want any grain. I'm tired of pigeons and tired of your story-telling. I don't believe there is a pigeon with a silver foot.

CUSTOMER. It's strange that the birds come to you, though, is it not?

BIANCA. They're just hungry. As I am.

CUSTOMER. So you won't be going to the Piazza tonight? What a pity.

BIANCA. Why?

CUSTOMER. Even now his gondola may be setting out over the sea. He may be lying even now on the cushions, trailing his long white hand in the water, his bright and sparkling gaze upon the shores and towers of Venice. I can almost see the small waves rippling over his ring. Listen——

(*Two female voices singing very softly.*)

VOICE. Moon and waves of the white lagoon
            Are bringing my love to land,
        And the stars fade as my love flashes
            The ring on his milk-white hand. . . .

CUSTOMER. Two *schei* for your cup.

BIANCA. Oh, I don't know what to say!

CUSTOMER. Two *schei,* and be off with you!

BIANCA. I wish I were strong enough to say no. But I can't! I can't! Give me the money, take the cup and go.

(*She thrusts the cup into the* CUSTOMER'*s hand. The* CUSTOMER *gives her the money, bestows the cup under her cloak and goes swiftly away. Blackout.*)

WAITER'S VOICE (*in darkness*). So Bianca ran off very fast indeed, very fast, so that she had to think about running and not about crying, and she ran through the little streets and the alleys and over the bridges but when she was half-way along the Mercerie, an old woman sprang up in her path.

(*Light shines on side of stage.* BIANCA *and the* BEGGAR WOMAN, *shapeless in rags, are confronting each other. The* BEGGAR *has her arms flung wide, to stop* BIANCA'*s progress.*)

BIANCA.   What are you doing? You mustn't stop me now.

BEGGAR.   You must help me, pretty *signorina*, for if nobody helps me my grandson will die.

BIANCA.   I can't help you. I don't know how. And I'm in a terrible hurry!

BEGGAR.   He must have the yellow medicine from the chemist, or he will die. He is only ten years old. And I have no money to buy the medicine. Only two *schei*, *signorina*, only two *schei*!

BIANCA.   I can't give it you—I can't! I have only two *schei* in the world and that is to buy me a lover.

BEGGAR.   My grandson is only ten years old and he is gasping for breath. Lover or no lover, you are alive, and you see the sun rise in the morning over the lagoon, and you know how nice bread is to eat and water is to drink, but tomorrow he will see nothing and know nothing, for ever and for ever. Please give me the money. You are good and kind. You would not see a child die, not for all the lovers in Christendom.

(BIANCA *hesitates for a moment. Then with a sob and a gasp, she tosses her last two schei to the ground and runs off. Black-out.*)

MARY'S VOICE.   The beggar woman was really the Customer, I suppose, testing Bianca out?

JOANNA'S VOICE. I always thought all this testing was rather mean, as a matter of fact.

WAITER'S VOICE. Yes, you are right, it was the Customer in disguise: and I agree this testing is, as you say, a little of a cheat. But as you say, Bianca behaved very well indeed, and gave all her money away.

JOANNA'S VOICE. What did she do then? Just go off home?

WAITER'S VOICE. No. Somehow, she couldn't bring herself to go home. She felt she was so near the Piazza that she might as well finish her journey. So she stepped into the Square and it was blazing with the moon. You could have read a newspaper by the light of it. You could also see the smallest tear on Bianca's cheek. And the first thing Bianca saw was that she was not alone.

> (*The lights go up on side of stage.* THE LOVER *in
> black cloak, three-corner hat and the grotesque
> Venetian mask, the bauta, stands feeding the
> pigeons.*
>
> *This scene is played both by him and* BIANCA *in
> mime, according to the description of the* WAITER.)

In the middle of the square was a young man, handsomely attired in tricorne hat and cloak, but she could not see his face, for he was wearing the famous Venetian mask, the *bauta*, which looks just a little frightening, don't you think? —But the gallants of those days used it for a disguise when they were off to meet ladies whom they should not meet.

And the whole square was alive with pigeons, flying about the young man's head, so that now and then, laughing, he had to beat them away; covering his arm like a muff of feathers, ebbing and flowing in a feathered sea about his

feet. Bianca watched him, hands clasped upon her heart:
suddenly he spoke.

LOVER. Why don't *you* feed them, too?

BIANCA. I can't. I haven't any grain.

LOVER. Can't you buy some?

BIANCA. I haven't any money. I gave it to a beggar
woman.

LOVER. Then I shall give you some of mine. Hold out
your right hand.

> (BIANCA *does so and he pours the grain into her palm;
> the miming action takes place as the female voices
> sing.*)

VOICES. Moon and waves of the white lagoon
> Are bringing my love to land;
> And the stars fade as my love flashes
> The ring on his milk-white hand.
> Serene he steps from the sill of the dawn
> And the smile that he saves for me
> Catches his eyes as St. Mark's catches
> The sun across the sea.

> (MIMING ACTION: *Young man moves slowly down-
> stage and stands with his arms folded.* BIANCA
> *thanks him for the grain, goes up-stage, and feeds
> the birds. First she kneels, encouraging them to
> come about her feet. One springs on to her finger.
> She rises very slowly from her knees, bearing the
> bird upwards. Then they crowd upon her.*)

BIANCA. Another, and another and another! I never saw
so many!

LOVER. Look for the silver foot!

BIANCA (*excitedly searching*). Have you got it, you

with the green breast? No. Rosy feet only. Have *you*?
You're a fine bird, a prince of birds, very fat. No. Don't
drive the others away, greedy! You're a pigeon in the
manger. You don't want to eat yourself, do you? And you
won't let your friends eat, either. You, now, come off my
shoulder, so that I can see you! Ah, I believe it's you!
Don't struggle, I mean to hold you tight—No. Not you.
Come on, come on, all of you . . . you, with the white
cross on your tail, show me your foot. . . . No. (*Cries out.*)
Oh! They've all gone, every one! Come back, come back!
Oh, they mustn't leave me now, they mustn't, they mustn't
. . . I knew it would be no good, I knew, I knew. And
they've all gone, and my grain is all gone.

LOVER.   You have one last single golden grain clinging
to your shawl.

(BIANCA *searches, finds it.*)

Put it on your palm. Hold it out. So. Now wait.

(*She stands quite still, her head raised, her palm outstretched.*)

SINGLE FEMALE VOICE (*singing*).
        Serene he steps from the sill of dawn
            And the smile that he saves for me
        Catches his eyes as St. Mark's catches——
BIANCA   (*crying out*). Look, here he comes!
WAITER'S VOICE.   A single bird flew down from the spire
of St. Mark's, circled Bianca's head, dropped lower and
fluttered about her hand, not perching, not perching, not
yet . . . feathers ruffled, eyes bright, not quite to be caught
. . . then . . .
BIANCA.   Ah! (*Her face is radiant. She watches the bird
as it lights upon her wrist and pecks at the single grain.*)

It has a silver foot! It is the pigeon with the silver foot!
He's flying away now . . . oh, don't fly away now . . . oh,
don't fly away, don't, don't . . .

> (*She stops short. There is a moment of complete
> silence. Then, as if compelled, she moves slowly
> towards the motionless young man.*)

BIANCA.   Take off your mask.

> (*He does not respond.*)

BIANCA.   Please. Please. Take off your mask.

> (*The* LOVER *raises his hands to his head. The mask
> falls at his feet.* BIANCA *can see his face, but the
> audience cannot.*)

(*Joyous.*)   It is you!

> (*He opens his arms wide and she runs into them. He
> bends his head to kiss her, then sweeps his cloak
> round her, obliterating her from view.*)

SINGLE FEMALE VOICE.

> And the smile that he saves for me
>   Catches his eyes as St. Mark's catches
> The sun across the sea.

> (*Black-out.*)

> (*The light goes up on the modern scene. The* WAITER,
> *smiling, indicates that the story has come to an
> end.*)

JOANNA.   So it was Mario after all, who was the real
lover all the time!

MARY.   And she found what she needed in him, the moral
being that what we most desire is often too close for us to
see it.

WAITER (*after a pause; briskly*). Not at all. It certainly wasn't Mario.

JOANNA ⎫
MARY ⎭ What?

WAITER. He married Caterina, Bertolo's daughter, went into business and was happy ever after.

MARY. Then who was the man in the mask?

WAITER (*patiently*). The lover she'd been promised, of course, handsome, proud and rich. You think poor young ladies never marry princes, don't you? Well, usually they don't. But Bianca did. And if you take the *vaporetto* along the Grand Canal you will see, not far from the Ca'd'Oro, to the left of it, the wonderful palace where they lived and died, always happy and always in love.

So there's hope for you, ladies!

Let me see . . . *trecento, quattrocento, cinquecento* . . . *sei cento*, if you please!

(MARY *pays him. The girls rise, collecting their belongings.*)

Grazie, signore, buona sera, and I wish you a prince apiece, for you see, it *can* be done!

(*The girls laugh, nod to him and stroll slowly off arm-in-arm,* MARY *whistling the song, as*

THE CURTAIN FALLS.)

SUNDAY COSTS FIVE PESOS
A MEXICAN FOLK COMEDY

by

JOSEPHINA NIGGLI

CHARACTERS

Fidel (who is in love with Berta)

Berta

Salome
Tonia   (Friends of Berta)

Celestina

SCENE: A housed-in square in the town of Four
Cornstalks (Las Cuatro Milpas) in Northern
Mexico.

TIME: Early one Sunday afternoon. The Present.

SUNDAY COSTS FIVE PESOS

THE SCENE: *A housed-in square in the town called Four Cornstalks in the northern part of Mexico.*

On the left of the square is the house of TONIA *with a door and a stoop. At the back is a wall cut neatly in half. The left side is the house of* BERTA, *and boasts not only a door but a barred window. On the right is a square arch from which dangles an iron lantern. This is the only exit to the rest of the town, for on the right side proper is the house of* SALOME. TONIA'S *house is pink, and* SALOME'S *is blue, while* BERTA'S *is content with being a sort of disappointed yellow. All three houses get their water from the well that is centre.*

It is early afternoon on Sunday, and all sensible people are sleeping, but through the arch comes FIDEL DURAN. *His straw hat in his hand, his hair plastered to his head with water, he thinks he is a very handsome sight indeed as he pauses, takes a small mirror from his pocket, fixes his neck bandanna—a beautiful purple one with orange spots, and shyly knocks at the door up left centre, then turns round with a broad grin on his face.*

BERTA *opens the door.* BERTA *is very pretty, but unfortunately she has a very high temper, possibly the result of her red hair. She wears a neat cotton dress and tennis shoes, blue ones. Her hands fastened on her hips, she stands and glares at* FIDEL.

BERTA.   Oh, so it is you!

FIDEL   (*beaming on her*).   A good afternoon to you, Berta.

BERTA   (*sniffing*).   A good afternoon indeed, and I bothered by fools at this hour of the day.

FIDEL   (*in amazement*).   Why, Berta! Are you angry with me?

BERTA   (*questioning heaven*).   He asks me if I am angry with him. Saints in Heaven, has he no memory?

FIDEL   (*puzzled*).   What have I done, Berta?

BERTA   (*sarcastically*).   Nothing, Fidel, nothing. That is the trouble. But if you come to this house again I will show you the palm of my hand, as I'm showing it to you now!

(*She slaps him, steps back inside the door, and slams it shut.*)

FIDEL   (*pounding on the door*).   Open the door, Berta. Open the door! I must speak to you!

(*The door of* SALOME's *house opens, and* SALOME *herself comes out with a small pitcher and begins drawing water from the well. She is twenty-eight, and so many years of hunting a husband have left her with an acid tongue.*)

SALOME.   And this is supposed to be a quiet street.

FIDEL   (*who dislikes her*).   You tend to your affairs, Salome, and I will tend to mine. (*He starts pounding again.*

He bleats like a young goat hunting for its mother.) Berta,
Berta.

BERTA (*opens the door again*). I will not have such
noises. Do you not realize that this is Sunday afternoon?
Have you no thoughts for decent people who are trying to
sleep?

FIDEL. Have you no thoughts for me?

BERTA. More than one. And none of them nice.

SALOME. I would call this a lover's quarrel.

BERTA. Would you indeed! (*She glares at* FIDEL.)
I would call it the impertinence of a wicked man!

FIDEL (*helplessly*). But what have I done?

SALOME. She loved him yesterday, and she will love him
tomorrow.

BERTA (*runs down to* SALOME). If I love him tomorrow,
may I lose the use of my tongue, yes, and my eyes and
ears, too.

FIDEL (*swinging* BERTA *to one side*). Is it fair, I ask
you, for a woman to smile at a man one day, and slap his
face the next? Is this the manner in which a promised bride
should treat her future husband?

SALOME (*grins and winks at him*). You could find yourself another bride.

BERTA (*angrily*). We do not need your advice, Salome
Molina. You and your long nose . . . sticking it in everyone's business.

SALOME (*her eyes flashing*). Is this an insult to me?
To me?

BERTA. And who are you to be above insults?

SALOME. I will not stay and listen to such words!

BERTA. Did I ask you to leave the safety of your house?

SALOME (*to* FIDEL). She has not even common politeness. I am going!

BERTA.   We shall adore your absence.

SALOME.   If this were not Sunday, I would slap your face for you.

BERTA   (*taunting*). The great Salome Molina, afraid of a Sunday fine.

FIDEL   (*wanting to be helpful*). You can fight each other tomorrow. There is no fine for weekdays.

SALOME.   You stay out of this argument, Fidel Duran.

FIDEL.   If you do not leave us I will never find out why Berta is angry with me. (*He jumps toward her.*)   Go away!

SALOME   (*jumps back, then tosses her head*). Very well. But the day will come when you will be glad of my company.

(*She goes indignantly into her house.*)

FIDEL   (*turns to* BERTA). Now, Berta.

BERTA   (*interrupting*). As for you, my fine rooster, go and play the bear to Celestina Garcia. She will appreciate you more than I.

FIDEL   (*with a guilty hand to his mouth*). So that is what it is.

BERTA   (*on the stoop of her own house*). That is all of it, and enough it is. Two times you walked around the plaza with the Celestina last night, and I sitting there on a bench having to watch you.

(*She goes into the house.*)

FIDEL.   (*speaking through the open door*). But it was a matter of business.

BERTA   (*enters with a broom and begins to sweep off the stoop*). Hah! Give me no such phrases.   And all of my friends thinking, "Poor Berta, with such a sweetheart." Do you think I have no pride?

FIDEL.   But it is that you do not understand. . . .

BERTA. I understand enough to know that all is over between us.

FIDEL. Berta, do not say that. I love you.

BERTA. So you say. And yet you roll the eye at any passing chicken.

FIDEL. Celestina is the daughter of Don Nimfo Garcia.

BERTA. She can be the daughter of the president for all of me. When you marry her, she will bring you a fine dowry, and there will be no more need of Fidel Duran trying to carve wooden doors.

FIDEL (*his pride wounded*). Trying? But I have carved them. Did I not do a new pair for the saloon?

BERTA. Aye, little doors . . . doors that amounted to no more than that . . . (*She snaps her fingers.*) Not for you the great doors of a church.

FIDEL. Why else do you think I was speaking with the Celestina?

BERTA (*stops sweeping*). What new manner of excuse is this?

FIDEL. That is why I came to speak with you. Sit down here on the step with me for a moment.

BERTA (*scandalized*). And have Salome and Tonia say that I am a wicked, improper girl!

FIDEL (*measuring a tiny space between his fingers*). Just for one little moment. They will see nothing.

BERTA (*sitting down*). Let the words tumble out of your mouth, one, two, three.

FIDEL (*sitting beside her*). Perhaps you do not know that the town of Topo Grande, thirty kilometres from here, is building a new church.

BERTA (*sniffs*). All the world knows that.

FIDEL. But did you know that Don Nimfo is secretly giving the money for the building of that church?

BERTA. Why?

FIDEL. He offered the money to the Blessed Virgin of Topo Grande if his rooster won the cock-fight. It did win, so now he is building the church.

BERTA (*not yet convinced*). How did you find out about this? Or has Don Nimfo suddenly looked upon you as a son, and revealed all his secrets to you?

FIDEL. Last night on the plaza the Celestina happened to mention it. With a bit of flattery I soon gained the whole story from her.

BERTA. So that is what you were talking about as you walked around the plaza? (*Standing.*) It must have taken a great deal of flattery to gain so much knowledge from her.

FIDEL (*stands*). Do you not realize what it means? They will need someone to carve the new doors.

(*He strikes a pleased attitude, expecting her to say, "But how wonderful, Fidel."*)

BERTA (*knowing very well what* FIDEL *expects, promptly turns away from him, her hand hiding a smile, as she says with innocent curiosity*). I wonder whom Don Nimfo will get? (*With the delight of discovery.*) Perhaps the Brothers Ochoa from Monterrey.

FIDEL (*crestfallen*). He might choose me.

BERTA. You? Hah!

FIDEL. And why not? Am I not the best wood-carver in the valley?

BERTA. So you say.

FIDEL. It would take three years to carve those doors and he would pay me every week. There would be enough to buy you a trousseau and enough left over for a house.

BERTA.　Did you tell all that to the Celestina?

FIDEL.　Of course not! Does a girl help a man buy a trousseau for another girl? That was why it had to appear as though I were rolling the eye at her. (*He is very pleased with his brilliance.*)

BERTA.　Your success was more than perfect. Today all the world knows that the Celestina has won Berta's man.

FIDEL.　But all the world does not know that Fidel Duran, who is I, myself, will carve those doors so as to buy a trousseau and house for Berta, my queen.

BERTA.　Precisely. All the world does not know this great thing. . . . (*Flaring out at him.*) And neither do I!

FIDEL.　Do you doubt me, pearl of my life?

BERTA.　Does the rabbit doubt the snake? Does the tree doubt the lightning? Do I doubt that you are a teller of tremendous lies? Speak not to me of cleverness. I know what my own eyes see, and I saw you flirting with the Celestina. Last night I saw you . . . and so did all the world!

FIDEL　(*beginning to grow angry*).　So that is how you trust me, your intended husband.

BERTA.　I would rather trust a hungry fox.

FIDEL.　Let me speak plainly, my little dove. Because we are to be married is no reason for me to enter a monastery.

BERTA.　And who says that we are to be married?

FIDEL　(*taken aback*).　Why . . . I said it.

BERTA.　Am I a dog to your heel that I must obey your every wish?

FIDEL　(*firmly*).　You are my future wife.

BERTA　(*laughs loudly*).　Am I indeed?

FIDEL.　Your mother has consented, and my father has spoken. The banns have been read in the church!

(He folds his arms with satisfaction.)

BERTA   *(screaming)*. Better to die without children than to be married to such as you.

FIDEL   *(screaming above her)*. We shall be married, within the month.

BERTA.   May this hand rot on my arm if I ever sign the marriage contract.

FIDEL.   Are you saying that you will not marry me?

BERTA.   With all my mouth I am saying it, and a good day to you.

> *(She steps inside the house and slams the door. Then immediately opens it and sticks her head out.)*

Tell that good news to that four-nosed shrew of a Celestina.

> *(She slams the door again.* FIDEL *puts on his hat and starts towards the archway, then runs down and pounds on* TONIA's *door, then runs across and pounds on* SALOME's. *In a moment both girls come out.* TONIA *is younger and smaller in size than either* SALOME *or* BERTA *and has a distressing habit of whining.)*

SALOME.   What is the meaning of this noise?

TONIA.   Is something wrong?

FIDEL.   I call you both to witness what I say. May I drop dead if I am ever seen in this street again!

> *(He settles his hat more firmly on his head, and with as much dignity as he can muster, he strides out through the arch. The girls stare after him, then at* BERTA's *door, then at each other. Both shrug, then with one accord they run up and begin knocking on the door.)*

SALOME. Berta!

TONIA. Berta, come out!

> (BERTA *enters. She is obviously trying to keep from crying.*)

SALOME. Has that fool of a sweetheart of yours lost his mind?

TONIA. What happened?

BERTA (*crying in earnest*). This day is blacker than a crow's wing. Oh, Salome!

> (*She flings both arms about the girl's neck and begins to wail loudly.* TONIA *and* SALOME *stare at each other, and then* TONIA *pats* BERTA *on the shoulder.*)

TONIA. Did you quarrel with Fidel?

SALOME. Of course she quarrelled with him. Any fool could see that.

BERTA. He will never come back to me. Never!

TONIA (*to* SALOME). Did she say anything about the Celestina to him?

SALOME (*to* BERTA). You should have kept your mouth shut on the outside of your teeth.

BERTA. A girl has her pride, and no Celestina is going to take any man of mine.

TONIA. But did she take him?

BERTA (*angrily to* TONIA). You take your face away from here!

SALOME. The only thing you can do now is to ask him to come back to you.

TONIA (*starting towards the archway*). I will go and get him.

BERTA (*clutches at her*). I will wither on my legs before I ask him to come back. He would never let me forget that

I had to beg him to marry me. (*She wails again.*)   And now he will marry the Celestina.

(TONIA *begins to cry with her.*)

TONIA.   There are other men.

BERTA.   My heart is with Fidel. My life is ruined.

SALOME   (*thoughtfully*). If we could bring him back . . . without his knowing Berta has sent for him . . . (*She sits on the edge of the well.*)

TONIA.   Miracles only happen in the church.

SALOME   (*catches her knee and begins to rock back and forth*). What could we tell him? What could we tell him?

TONIA.   You be careful, Salome, or you will fall in the well. Then we will all have to go into mourning, and Berta cannot get married at all if she is in mourning.

SALOME   (*snaps her fingers*). You could fall down the well, Berta! That would bring him back.

BERTA   (*firmly*). I will not fall down the well and drown for any man, not even Fidel.

TONIA.   What good would bringing him back do if Berta were dead?

SALOME.   Now that is a difficulty. (*She begins to pace up and down.*) If you are dead, you cannot marry Fidel. If you are not dead, he will not come back. The only thing left for you is to die an old maid.

TONIA.   That would be terrible.

BERTA   (*wailing*). My life is ruined. Completely ruined.

SALOME   (*with sudden determination*). Why? Why should it be?

TONIA   (*with awe*). Salome has had a thought.

BERTA.   You do not know what a terrible thing it is to lose the man you love.

SALOME.   I am fixing up your life, not mine. Suppose . . . suppose you did fall in the well.

BERTA.   I tell you I will not do it.

SALOME.   Not really, but suppose he thought you did. What then?

BERTA.   You mean . . . Pretend? But that is a sin. The priest would give me ten days' penance at confessional.

SALOME   (*flinging out her hands*).   Ten days' penance or a life without a husband. Which do you choose?

TONIA.   I will tell you. She chooses a husband. What do we do, Salome?

SALOME.   You run and find this carver of doors, tell him that a great scandal has happened . . . that Berta has fallen in the well.

TONIA   (*whose dramatic imagination has begun to work*). Because she could not live without him . . .

BERTA.   You tell him that and I will scratch out both your eyes!

TONIA.   On Sunday?

BERTA   (*sullenly*).   On any day.

SALOME.   Tell him that Berta has fallen in the well, and that you think she is dying.

TONIA.   Is that all?

BERTA.   Is that not enough?

SALOME   (*entranced with the idea*).   Oh, it will be a great scene, with Berta so pale in her bed, and Fidel kneeling in tears beside her.

BERTA.   I want you to know that I am a modest girl.

SALOME   (*irritated*).   You can lie down on the floor, then. (*Glaring at* TONIA.) What are you standing there for? Run!

TONIA   (*starts towards the archway, then comes back*). But . . . where will I go?

SALOME. To the place where all men go with a broken heart . . . the saloon. Are you going to stand there all day?

(TONIA *gives a little gasp and runs out through the arch.*)

BERTA. I do not like this idea. If Fidel finds out it is a trick, he will be angrier than ever.

SALOME. But if he does not find out the truth until after you are married . . . what difference will it make?

BERTA. He might beat me.

SALOME. Leave that worry until after you are married. (*Inspecting* BERTA.) Now how will we make you look pale? Have you any flour? Corn-meal might do.

BERTA. No! No! I will not do it.

SALOME. Now Berta, be reasonable.

BERTA. If I had really fallen down the well, it would be different. But I did not fall down it.

SALOME. Do you not want Fidel to come back to you? Are you not in love with him?

BERTA. Yes, I do love him. And I will play no tricks on him. If he loves the Celestina better than he does me . . . (*with great generosity*) he can marry her.

SALOME (*pleading with much idiocy*). But Tonia has gone down to get him. If he comes back and finds you alive . . . he will be angrier than ever.

BERTA (*firmly*). This is your idea. You can get out of it the best way you can. But Fidel will not see me lying down on a bed, nor on a floor, nor any place else.

SALOME. Then there is only one thing to do.

BERTA. What is that?

SALOME. You will go into the house, and I will tell him that you are too sick to see him.

BERTA. That will be just as bad as the other.

SALOME. How can it be? Then if he finds out it is a trick, he will blame me, and you can pretend you knew nothing of it. I do not care how angry he is. I do not want to marry him.

BERTA (*with pleased excitement*). Then he could not be angry with me, could he? I mean if he thought I had nothing to do with it? And I would not have to do penance either, would I?

SALOME. Not one day of penance. Tonia should have found him by now. (*She goes to the arch and peers through.*) Here they come . . . and Fidel is running half a block in front of her.

BERTA (*joyously*). Then he does love me!

SALOME. Into the house with you. You can watch through the window.

BERTA (*on stoop*). Now, remember, if he gets angry, this was your idea.

SALOME (*clasps her hands*). And what a beautiful idea it is!

> (BERTA *disappears into the house.* SALOME *looks about her, then dashes over to her own stoop, sits down, flings her shawl over her face, and begins to moan loudly, rocking back and forth. In a moment* FIDEL *dashes through the arch, and stops, out of breath, at seeing* SALOME.)

FIDEL (*gasping*). Berta!

SALOME (*whose moaning grows louder*). Poor darling, poor darling. She was so young.

FIDEL (*desperately.*) She is . . . she is dead?

SALOME (*wailing*). She will make such a beautiful corpse. Poor darling. Poor darling.

(*Tonia, exhausted and out of breath, has reached the arch.*)

TONIA (*looks about her in astonishment*). Why, where is Berta? Did she go into the house?

SALOME (*in normal tones*). Of course she went into the house, you fool. Did she not jump down the well? (*Remembering* FIDEL.) Poor darling.

TONIA (*blankly*). Did she really jump down it? I thought she just fell in by accident.

SALOME (*grimly*). Are you telling this story . . . or am I? (*Wailing.*) Now she can never go to the plaza again.

(FIDEL *looks helplessly from* TONIA, *who cannot quite get the details of the story straight, to* SALOME, *who is having a beautiful time mourning.*)

FIDEL. Where is she? I want to see her.

'TONIA (*coming out of her trance*). She is right in here. Did you say she was on the bed or on the floor, Salome?

SALOME (*getting between them and* BERTA's *door*). You don't want to see her, Fidel. You know how people look after they've been drowned.

TONIA. But he was supposed to see her. That was why you sent . . .

SALOME (*glaring at her*). Tonia, dear, suppose that you let me tell the story. After all, I was here and you were not.

FIDEL (*exploding*). For the love of the saints, tell me! Is she dead?

SALOME (*thinking this over*). Well . . . not exactly.

FIDEL. You mean . . . you mean there is hope?

SALOME. I would say there was great hope.

FIDEL (*takes off his hat and mops his face*). What can I do? Oh, if I could only see her . . .

SALOME. If you would go to the church and light a candle to Our Blessed Lady and ask her to forgive you for getting angry with Berta . . . perhaps things will arrange themselves.

FIDEL. Do you think she will get well soon?

SALOME. With a speed that will amaze you.

FIDEL. I will go down and light the candle right now.

(*As he turns to leave, who should come through the archway but* CELESTINA GARCIA. *She can match temper for temper with* BERTA *any day, and right now she is on the war-path. Brushing past these three as though they did not exist, she goes up to* BERTA'*s door and pounds on it.*)

CELESTINA. I dare you to come out and call this Celestina Garcia a four-nosed shrew to her face.

SALOME (*trying to push* FIDEL *through the arch*). You had best run to the church.

FIDEL (*pushing past her and going up to* CELESTINA). How dare you speak like that to a poor drowned soul?

SALOME (*to* CELESTINA). Why do you not go away? We never needed you so little.

CELESTINA. So she is pretending to be drowned, eh? Is that her coward's excuse?

BERTA (*through window*). Who dares to call Berta Cantu a coward?

CELESTINA. You know well enough who calls you, and I the daughter of Don Nimfo Garcia.

TONIA. Ai, Salome! And now Fidel will know that Berta was not drowned at all.

FIDEL (*who has been listening to this conversation with growing surprise and suspicion, now turns furiously towards*

BERTA's *house*). Not drowned, eh? So this was a trick to bring me back, eh? I am through with your tricks, you hear me? Through with them!

BERTA (*through window*). You stay right there until I come out. (*She disappears from view.*)

FIDEL (*turning to Salome*). I see your hand in this.

SALOME. The more fool you to be taken in by a woman's tricks.

CELESTINA. What care I for tricks? No woman is going to call me names!

BERTA (*coming through the door*). You keep silence, Celestina Garcia. I will deal with you in a minute. And as for you, Fidel Duran . . .

FIDEL (*stormily*). As for me, I am finished with all women. The world will see me no more. I will enter a monastery and carve as many doors as I like. Do you hear me, Berta Cantu?

BERTA (*putting both hands over her ears*). What do I care for your quack quack, quack!

FIDEL. Now she calls me a duck. Good afternoon to you!

(*He stalks out with wounded dignity.*)

CELESTINA (*catching* BERTA *by the shoulder and swinging her round*). I ask you again: Did you call me a four-nosed shrew?

BERTA. I did, and I will repeat it with the greatest of pleasure. You are a four-nosed shrew and a three-eyed frog!

CELESTINA. I have always looked on you as my friend . . . you pink-toed cat!

BERTA. And I have always trusted you . . . you sly robber of bridegrooms!

(*She raises her hand to slap Celestina.* SALOME *catches it.*)

SALOME. This is Sunday, Berta! And Sunday costs five pesos.

TONIA. If you had to pay a fine for starting a fight on top of losing Fidel . . . Ay, that would be terrible.

(BERTA *and* CELESTINA *glare at each other, and then slowly begin to circle each other, spitting out their insults as they do so.*)

CELESTINA. It is my honour that is making me fight, or I would wait until tomorrow.

BERTA. If I had five pesos to throw away, I would pull out your dangling tongue . . . leaving only the flapping roots.

CELESTINA. Ha! I make a nose at your words.

BERTA. As for you . . . you eater of ugly-smelling cheese . . .

(*They jump at each other, but remember the penalty just in time and pull back. Again they begin to circle round, contenting themselves with making faces at each other.* SALOME *suddenly clasps her hands.*)

SALOME. You are both certain that you want to fight today?

CELESTINA. Why else do you think I came here?

BERTA. These insults have gone too far to stop now.

SALOME. The only thing that stands in the way is the five pesos for the Sunday fine.

TONIA. And five pesos is a lot of money.

SALOME. Then the only thing to do is to play the fingers.

CELESTINA. What?

BERTA. Eh?

SALOME. Precisely. Whoever loses strikes the first blow
and pays this fine. Then you can fight as much as you like.

TONIA (*with awed admiration*). Ay, Salome, you have
so many brains.

CELESTINA (*doubtfully*). It is a big risk.

BERTA (*shrugging*). Perhaps you are afraid of taking
a risk.

CELESTINA. I am not afraid of anything. But Tonia will
have to be the judge. Salome is too clever.

BERTA. Very well. But Salome has to stand behind you
to see that you do not cheat. I would not trust you any
more than I would a mouse near a piece of fresh bacon.

CELESTINA (*pulls back her clenched fist, then thinks
better of it, and speaks with poor grace*). Very well.

> (CELESTINA *and* BERTA *stand facing each other.*
> TONIA *stands between them up on the stoop.*
> SALOME *stands behind* CELESTINA.)

TONIA (*feeling a little nervous over this great honour of
judging*). Both arms behind your backs. (*The girls link
their arms behind them.*) Now, when I drop my hand, Berta
will guess first as Celestina brings her fingers forward. The
first girl to guess correctly twice wins. Are you ready? (*All
nod.*) I am going to drop my arm.

SALOME. Celestina, put out your fingers before Berta
guesses. We will have no cheating.

CELESTINA (*suddenly*). Very well.

> (*She puts out two fingers behind her, and* SALOME,
> *seeing this, raises up her arm with two fingers ex-
> tended, opening and closing them scissors fashion.*
> BERTA *frowns a little as she looks up at the signal
> and* CELESTINA *seeing this, swings round and looks*

at SALOME, *who promptly grins warmly and pretends to be waving at* BERTA. CELESTINA *then looks at* TONIA.)

BERTA. Very well.

CELESTINA   (*guessing as* BERTA *swings her arm forward*). Three.

(BERTA *triumphantly holds up one finger. Biting her lip,* CELESTINA *starts to swing forward her own arm.* SALOME, *intent on signalling* BERTA, *holds up her own five fingers spread wide, and does not notice until too late that* CELESTINA *has swung round to watch her.*)

CELESTINA   (*screaming*). So I cheat, eh?   (*With that she gives* SALOME *a resounding slap on the cheek.*)

(*The next moment the two women are mixed up in a beautiful, howling, grunting fight while* TONIA *and* BERTA, *wide-eyed, cling together and give the two women as much space as possible. Let it be understood that this is only a fight of kicking, hairpulling and scratching. There is no man involved, nor a point of honour. Rather a matter of angry pride. So the two are not attempting to mutilate each other. They are simply gaining satisfaction. The grand finale comes when* CELESTINA *knocks* SALOME *to the ground and sits on her.*)

CELESTINA   (*breathing hard*). There! That was worth five pesos.

TONIA.   You have to pay it. And Don Nimfo will be angry with you.

CELESTINA   (*pulling herself to her feet*). I am too tired

to fight any more now, but I will be back next Tuesday,
Berta, and then I will beat you up.

BERTA   (*sniffing*). If you can.

CELESTINA   (*warningly*). And there is no fine on
Tuesday.

BERTA.   Come any day you like. I will be ready for you.

TONIA   (*to* CELESTINA). You should be ashamed to fight.

CELESTINA.   Who are you to talk to me? (*She stamps
her foot at* TONIA, *who jumps behind* BERTA.) Good afternoon, my brave little rabbits!

> (*She staggers out as straight as she can, but as she
> reaches the archway she feels a twinge of agony
> and is forced to limp. By this time* SALOME *has
> gathered together what strength she has left, and
> she slowly stands up. Once erect, she looks at*
> BERTA *and* TONIA *as though she were considering
> boiling in oil too good for them.*)

SALOME   (*with repressed fury*). My friends. My very
good friends.

TONIA   (*frightened*). Now, Salome . . .

SALOME   (*screaming*). Do not speak to me! Either of
you! (*She manages to get to the door of her house.*) When
I need help, do you give me aid? No! But just you wait . . .
both of you!

TONIA.   What are you going to do?

SALOME.   I am going to wait for a week-day, and then
I am going to beat up both of you at once. One (*she takes
a deep breath*) with each hand! (*She nearly falls through
the door of her house.*)

BERTA   (*with false bravado*). Who is afraid of her?

TONIA.   I am. Salome is very strong. It is all your fault

If you had not gotten mad at Fidel, this would not have happened.

BERTA (*snapping at her*). You leave Fidel out of this.

TONIA (*beginning to cry*). When Salome beats me up, that will be your fault, too.

BERTA. Stop crying!

TONIA. I am not a good fighter, but I can tell Fidel the truth about how you would not jump down the well to win him back.

BERTA. You open your mouth to Fidel, and I will push you in the well.

TONIA. You will not have strength enough to push a baby in the well when they get through with you.

BERTA. Get out! Get out of here!

(*She stamps her foot at* TONIA *and the girl, frightened, gives a squeak and runs into her own house.* BERTA *looks after her, then, beginning to sniffle, she goes over and sits on the well. She acts like a child who has been told that it is not proper for little girls to cry, and she is very much in need of a handkerchief. Just then,* FIDEL *sticks his head round the arch.*)

FIDEL (*once more the plaintive goat*). Berta.

(BERTA *half jumps, then pretends not to hear him.* FIDEL *enters cautiously, not taking his eyes off* BERTA's *stiff back. He moves round at the back, skirts* TONIA's *house, then works his way round to her.*)

Berta.

BERTA (*sniffing*). What is it?

FIDEL (*circling the back of the well*). Are you crying, Berta?

BERTA   (*stubbornly*). No!

FIDEL   (*sitting beside her*). Yes, you are, I can see you crying.

BERTA.   If you can see, why do you ask, then?

FIDEL.   I am sorry we quarrelled, Berta.

BERTA.   Are you?

FIDEL.   Are you sorry?

BERTA.   No!

FIDEL.   I was hoping you were, because . . . do you know whom I saw on the plaza?

BERTA.   Grandfather Devil.

FIDEL.   Don Nimfo himself.

BERTA.   Perhaps you saw the Celestina too.

FIDEL   (*placatingly*). Now, Berta, you know I do not care if I never see the Celestina again. (*He pulls out a handkerchief and extends it to her.*) Here, wipe your face with this.

BERTA.   I have a handkerchief of my own. (*Nevertheless she takes it, and wipes her eyes and then blows her nose.*)

FIDEL.   Don Nimfo said I could carve the church doors for him. But he said I would have to move to Topo Grande to work on them. He said I had to leave right away.

BERTA   (*perking up her interest*). You mean . . . move right away from here?

FIDEL.   And I was wondering if we could get married tomorrow. I know this is very sudden, Berta, but after all, think how long I have waited to carve a church door.

BERTA.   Tomorrow. (*She looks towards* SALOME's *house.*) They would both be too sore to do anything by tomorrow.

FIDEL   (*too concerned with his own plans to hear what she is saying*). Of course, I know that you may not be able to forgive me . . .

BERTA.   Fidel, I want you to understand that if I do marry you tomorrow . . . that means we will leave here tomorrow, eh?

FIDEL.   Ay, yes. I have to be in Topo Grande on Tuesday.

BERTA.   I hope you will always understand what a great thing I have done for you. It is not every girl who would forgive so easily as I.

FIDEL   (*humbly*). Indeed, I know that, Berta.

BERTA.   Are you quite sure that we will leave here tomorrow?

FIDEL.   Quite sure.

BERTA.   Very well. I will marry you.

FIDEL   (*joyfully*). Berta!

(*He bends forward to kiss her. But she jumps up.*)

BERTA.   Just a moment. We are not married yet. Do you think that I am just any girl that you can kiss me . . . like that! (*She snaps her fingers.*)

FIDEL   (*humbly*). I thought . . . just this once . . .

BERTA   (*gravely thoughtful*). Well, perhaps . . . just this once . . . you may kiss my hand.

As he kisses it,

THE CURTAINS CLOSE

THE HAPPY JOURNEY

by

THORNTON WILDER

CHARACTERS

The Stage Manager

Ma Kirby

Arthur (thirteen)

Caroline (fifteen)

Pa (Elmer) Kirby

Beulah (twenty-two)

SCENE: No scenery is required for this play. The idea
is that no place is being represented.

THE HAPPY JOURNEY

SCENE: *As the curtain rises the* STAGE MANAGER *is leaning lazily against the proscenium pillar at the left. He is smoking.* ARTHUR *is playing marbles down centre in pantomime.* CAROLINE *is way up left talking to some girls who are invisible to us.* MA KIRBY *is anxiously putting on her hat (real) before an imaginary mirror up right.*

MA. Where's your pa? Why isn't he here? I declare we'll never get started.

ARTHUR. Ma, where's my hat? I guess I don't go if I can't find my hat. (*Still playing marbles.*)

MA. Go out into the hall and see if it isn't there. Where's Caroline gone to now, the plagued child?

ARTHUR. She's out waitin' in the street talkin' to the Jones girls.—I just looked in the hall a thousand times, Ma, and it isn't there. (*He spits for good luck before a difficult shot and mutters:*) Come on, baby.

MA. Go and look again, I say. Look carefully.

(ARTHUR *rises, reluctantly, crosses right, turns round, returns swiftly to his game centre, flinging himself*

This play is included in this anthology by permission of the author and of Messrs. Longmans, Green & Co. Limited, 48, Grosvenor Street, London, W.1, to whom all requests for quotation or performance of any kind should be referred.

*on the floor with a terrible impact and starts shoot-
ing an aggie.)*

ARTHUR.   No, Ma, it's not there.

MA   *(serenely)*. Well, you don't leave Newark without
that hat, make up your mind to that. I don't go no journeys
with a hoodlum.

ARTHUR.   Aw, Ma!

> (MA *comes down right to the footlights, pulls up an
> imaginary window and talks toward the audience.)*

MA   *(calling)*. Oh, Mrs. Schwartz!

THE STAGE MANAGER   *(down left. Consulting his script)*.
Here I am, Mrs. Kirby. Are you going yet?

MA.   I guess we're going in just a minute. How's the
baby?

THE STAGE MANAGER.   She's all right now. We slapped
her on the back and she spat it up.

MA.   Isn't that fine!—Well, now, if you'll be good enough
to give the cat a saucer of milk in the morning and the
evening, Mrs. Schwartz, I'll be ever so grateful to you.—
Oh, good afternoon, Mrs. Hobmeyer!

THE STAGE MANAGER.   Good afternoon, Mrs. Kirby, I
hear you're going away.

MA   *(modest)*. Oh, just for three days, Mrs. Hobmeyer,
to see my married daughter, Beulah, in Camden. Elmer's
got his vacation week from the laundry early this year, and
he's just the best driver in the world.

> (CAROLINE *comes down stage right and stands by
> her mother.)*

THE STAGE MANAGER.   Is the whole family going?

MA.   Yes, all four of us that's here. The change ought

to be good for the children. My married daughter was down-right sick a while ago——

THE STAGE MANAGER. Tchk—tchk—tchk! Yes. I remember you tellin' us.

MA. (*with feeling*). And I just want to go down and see the child. I ain't seen her since then. I just won't rest easy in my mind without I see her. (*To Caroline.*) Can't you say good afternoon to Mrs. Hobmeyer?

CAROLINE (*lowers her eyes and says woodenly*). Good afternoon, Mrs. Hobmeyer.

THE STAGE MANAGER. Good afternoon, dear—Well, I'll wait and beat these rugs until after you're gone, because I don't want to choke you. I hope you have a good time and find everything all right.

MA. Thank you, Mrs. Hobmeyer, I hope I will.—Well, I guess that milk for the cat is all, Mrs. Schwartz, if you're sure you don't mind. If anything should come up, the key to the back door is hanging by the ice-box.

CAROLINE. Ma! Not so loud.

ARTHUR. Everybody can hear yuh.

MA. Stop pullin' my dress, children. (*In a loud whisper.*) The key to the back door I'll leave hangin' by the ice-box and I'll leave the screen door unhooked.

THE STAGE MANAGER. Now have a good trip, dear, and give my love to Beuhly.

MA. I will, and thank you a thousand times. (*She lowers the window, turns up-stage and looks around.* CAROLINE *goes left and vigorously rubs her cheeks.* MA *occupies herself with the last touches of packing.*) What can be keeping your pa?

ARTHUR (*who has not left his marbles*). I can't find my hat, Ma.

(*Enter* ELMER *holding a cap, up right.*)

ELMER. Here's Arthur's hat. He musta left it in the car Sunday.

MA. That's a mercy. Now we can start.—Caroline Kirby, what you done to your cheeks?

CAROLINE (*defiant-abashed*). Nothin'.

MA. If you've put anything on 'em, I'll slap you.

CAROLINE. No, Ma, of course I haven't. (*Hanging her head.*) I just rubbed 'm to make 'm red. All the girls do that at High School when they're goin' places.

MA. Such silliness I never saw. Elmer, what kep' you?

ELMER (*always even-voiced and always looking out a little anxiously through his spectacles*). I just went to the garage and had Charlie give a last look at it, Kate.

MA. I'm glad you did. (*Collecting two pieces of imaginary luggage and starting for the door.*) I wouldn't like to have no breakdown miles from anywhere. Now we can start. Arthur, put those marbles away. Anybody'd think you didn't want to go on a journey, to look at yuh.

> (*They go out through the "hall". MA opens an imaginary door down right. PA, CAROLINE and ARTHUR go through it. MA follows, taking time to lock the door, hang the key by the "ice-box". They turn up at an abrupt angle, going up-stage. As they come to the steps from the back porch, each, arriving at a given point, starts bending his knees lower and lower to denote going downstairs, and find themselves in the street. The STAGE MANAGER moves from the right the automobile. It is right centre of the stage, seen partially at an angle, its front pointing down centre.*)

ELMER   (*coming forward*). Here, you boys, you keep away from that car.

MA.   Those Sullivan boys put their heads into everything.

> (*They get into the car,* ELMER's *hands hold an imaginary steering wheel and continually shift gears.* MA *sits beside him.* ARTHUR *is behind him and* CAROLINE *is behind* MA.)

CAROLINE   (*standing up in the back seat, waving, self-consciously*). Good-bye, Mildred. Good-bye, Helen.

THE STAGE MANAGER   (*having returned to his position by the left proscenium*). Good-bye, Caroline. Good-bye, Mrs. Kirby. I hope y' have a good time.

MA.   Good-bye, girls.

THE STAGE MANAGER.   Good-bye, Kate. The car looks fine.

MA.   (*looking upward toward a window right*). Oh, good-bye, Emma! (*Modestly.*) We think it's the best little Chevrolet in the world.—(*Looking up toward the left.*) Oh, good-bye, Mrs. Adler!

THE STAGE MANAGER.   What, are you going away, Mrs. Kirby?

MA.   Just for three days, Mrs. Adler, to see my married daughter in Camden.

THE STAGE MANAGER.   Have a good time.

> (*Now* MA, CAROLINE, *and the* STAGE MANAGER *break out into a tremendous chorus of good-byes. The whole street is saying good-bye.* ARTHUR *takes out his pea shooter and lets fly happily into the air. There is a lurch or two and they are off.*)

ARTHUR   (*leaning forward in sudden fright*). Pa! Pa! Don't go by the school. Mr. Biedenbach might see us!

MA. I don't care if he does see us. I guess I can take my children out of school for one day without having to hide down back streets about it. (ELMER *nods to a passer-by.* MA, *without sharpness.*) Who was that you spoke to, Elmer?

ELMER. That was the fellow who arranges our banquets down to the Lodge, Kate.

MA. Is he the one who had to buy four hundred steaks? (PA *nods.*) I declare, I'm glad I'm not him.

ELMER. The air's getting better already. Take deep breaths, children.

(*They inhale noisily.*)

ARTHUR (*pointing to a sign and indicating that it gradually goes by*). Gee, it's almost open fields already. "Weber and Heilbronner Suits for Well-dressed Men". Ma, can I have one of them some day?

MA. If you graduate with good marks perhaps your father'll let you have one for graduation.

(*Pause. General gazing about, then sudden lurch.*)

CAROLINE (*whining*). Oh, Pa! do we have to wait while that whole funeral goes by?

(ELMER *takes off his hat.* MA *cranes forward with absorbed curiosity.*)

MA (*not sharp and bossy*). Take off your hat, Arthur. Look at your father.—Why, Elmer, I do believe that's a lodge-brother of yours. See the banner? I suppose this is the Elizabeth branch. (ELMER *nods.* MA *sighs: tchk—tchk —tchk. The children lean forward and all watch the funeral in silence, growing momentarily more solemnized. After a pause,* MA *continues almost dreamily but not sentimentally.*) Well, we haven't forgotten the funeral that we went on, have we? We haven't forgotten our good Harold. He gave his life for his country, we mustn't forget that. (*There is another pause; with cheerful resignation.*) Well, we'll all hold up the traffic for a few minutes some day.

THE CHILDREN (*very uncomfortable*). Ma!

MA (*without self-pity*). Well, I'm "ready", children. I hope everybody in this car is "ready". And I pray to go first, Elmer. Yes.

(ELMER *touches her hand.*)

CAROLINE. Ma, everybody's looking at you.

ARTHUR. Everybody's laughing at you.

MA. Oh, hold your tongues! I don't care what a lot of silly people in Elizabeth, New Jersey, think of me.—Now we can go on. That's the last.

(*There is another lurch and the car goes on.*)

CAROLINE (*looking at a sign and turning as she passes it*). "Fit-Rite Suspenders. The Working Man's Choice". Pa, why do they spell Rite that way?

ELMER. So that it'll make you stop and ask about it, Missy.

CAROLINE. Papa, you're teasing me.—Ma, why do they say "Three Hundred Rooms Three Hundred Baths"?

ARTHUR. "Miller's Spaghetti: The Family's Favorite Dish". Ma, why don't you ever have spaghetti?

MA. Go along, you'd never eat it.

ARTHUR. Ma, I like it now.

CAROLINE (*with gesture*). Yum-yum. It looked wonderful up there. Ma, make some when we get home?

MA (*dryly*). "The management is always happy to receive suggestions. We aim to please."

(*The children scream with laughter. Even* ELMER
smiles. MA *remains modest.*)

ELMER. Well, I guess no one's complaining, Kate. Everybody knows you're a good cook.

MA. I don't know whether I'm a good cook or not, but I know I've had practice. At least I've cooked three meals a day for twenty-five years.

ARTHUR. Aw, Ma, you went out to eat once in a while.

MA. Yes. That made it a leap year

(*The children laugh again.*)

CAROLINE (*in an ecstasy of well-being puts her arms round her mother*). Ma, I love going out in the country like this. Let's do it often, Ma.

MA. Goodness, smell that air, will you! It's got the whole ocean in it.—Elmer, drive careful over that bridge. This must be New Brunswick we're coming to.

ARTHUR (*after a slight pause*). Ma, when is the next comfort station?

MA (*unruffled*). You don't want one. You just said that to be awful.

CAROLINE (*shrilly*). Yes, he did, Ma. He's terrible. He says that kind of thing right out in school and I want to sink through the floor, Ma. He's terrible.

MA. Oh, don't get so excited about nothing, Miss Proper! I guess we're all yewman beings in this car, at least as far as I know. And, Arthur, you try and be a gentleman.—Elmer, don't run over that collie dog. (*She follows the dog with her eyes.*) Looked kinda peaked to me. Needs a good honest bowl of leavings. Pretty dog, too. (*Her eyes fall on a billboard at the right.*) That's a pretty advertisement for Chesterfield cigarettes, isn't it? Looks like Beulah, a little.

ARTHUR. Ma?

MA. Yes.

ARTHUR (*"route" rhymes with "out"*). Can't I take a paper route with the *Newark Daily Post*?

MA. No, you cannot. No, sir. I hear they make the paper-boys get up at four-thirty in the morning. No son of mine is going to get up at four-thirty every morning, not if it's to make a million dollars. Your *Saturday Evening Post* route on Thursday mornings is enough.

ARTHUR. Aw, Ma.

MA. No, sir. No son of mine is going to get up at four-thirty and miss the sleep God meant him to have.

ARTHUR (*sullenly*). Hhm! Ma's always talking about God. I guess she got a letter from Him this morning.

MA (*outraged*). Elmer, stop that automobile this minute. I don't go another step with anybody that says things like that. Arthur, you get out of this car. (ELMER *stops the car*.) Elmer, you give him a dollar bill. He can go back to Newark by himself. I don't want him.

ARTHUR. What did I say? There wasn't anything terrible about that.

ELMER. I didn't hear what he said, Kate.

MA. God has done a lot of things for me and I won't have Him made fun of by anybody. Get out of this car this minute.

CAROLINE. Aw, Ma,—don't spoil the ride.

MA. No.

ELMER. We might as well go on, Kate, since we've got started. I'll talk to the boy tonight.

MA (*slowly conceding*). All right, if you say so, Elmer.
(ELMER *starts the car*.)

ARTHUR (*frightened*). Aw, Ma, that wasn't so terrible.

MA. I don't want to talk about it. I hope your father washes your mouth out with soap and water.—Where'd we all be if I started talking about God like that, I'd like to know! We'd be in the speak-easies and night-clubs and places like that, that's where we'd be.

CAROLINE (*after a very slight pause*). What did he say, Ma? I didn't hear what he said.

MA. I don't want to talk about it.

(*They drive on in silence for a moment, the shocked silence after a scandal.*)

ELMER. I'm going to stop and give the car a little water, I guess.

MA. All right, Elmer. You know best.

ELMER (*turns the wheel and stops; as to a garage hand*). Could I have a little water in the radiator—to make sure?

THE STAGE MANAGER (*in this scene alone he lays aside his script and enters into a role seriously*). You sure can. (*He punches the left front tire.*) Air all right? Do you need any oil or gas? (*Goes up round car.*)

ELMER. No, I think not. I just got fixed up in Newark.

(THE STAGE MANAGER *carefully pours some water into the hood.*)

MA. We're on the right road for Camden, are we?

THE STAGE MANAGER (*coming down on right side of car*). Yes, keep straight ahead. You can't miss it. You'll be in Trenton in a few minutes. Camden's a great town, lady, believe me.

MA. My daughter likes it fine—my married daughter.

THE STAGE MANAGER. Ye'? It's a great burg all right. I guess I think so because I was born near there.

MA. Well, well. Your folks still live there?

THE STAGE MANAGER (*standing with one foot on the rung of* MA's *chair. They have taken a great fancy to one another.*) No, my old man sold the farm and they built a factory on it. So the folks moved to Philadelphia.

MA. My married daughter Beulah lives there because her husband works in the telephone company.—Stop pokin' me, Caroline!—We're all going down to see her for a few days.

THE STAGE MANAGER. Ye'?

MA. She's been sick, you see, and I just felt I had to go and see her. My husband and my boy are going to stay at the Y.M.C.A. I hear they've got a dormitory on the top floor that's real clean and comfortable. Had you ever been there?

THE STAGE MANAGER. No. I'm Knights of Columbus myself.

MA. Oh.

THE STAGE MANAGER. I used to play basketball at the Y though. It looked all right to me. (*He reluctantly moves away and pretends to examine the car again.*) Well, I guess you're all set now, lady. I hope you have a good trip; you can't miss it.

EVERYBODY. Thanks. Thanks a lot. Good luck to you. (*Jolts and lurches.*)

MA (*with a sigh*). The world's full of nice people.— That's what I call a nice young man.

CAROLINE (*earnestly*). Ma, you oughtn't to tell 'm all everything about yourself.

MA. Well, Caroline, you do your way and I'll do mine. —He looked kinda pale to me. I'd like to feed him up for a few days. His mother lives in Philadelphia and I expect he eats at those dreadful Greek places.

CAROLINE. I'm hungry. Pa, there's a hot-dog stand. K'n I have one?

ELMER. We'll all have one, eh, Kate? We had such an early lunch.

MA. Just as you think best, Elmer.

(ELMER *stops the car.*)

ELMER. Arthur, here's half a dollar.—Run over and see what they have. Not too much mustard either.

(ARTHUR *descends from the car and goes off-stage right.* MA *and* CAROLINE *get out and walk a bit, up-stage and to the left.* CAROLINE *keeps at her mother's right.*)

MA. What's that flower over there?—I'll take some of those to Beulah.

CAROLINE. It's just a weed, Ma.

MA. I like it.—My, look at the sky, wouldya! I'm glad I was born in New Jersey. I've always said it was the best state in the Union. Every state has something no other state has got.

(*Presently* ARTHUR *returns with his hands full of imaginary hot-dogs which he distributes. First to his father, next to* CAROLINE, *who comes forward to meet him, and lastly to his mother. He is still very much cast down by the recent scandal, and as he approaches his mother says falteringly:*)

ARTHUR. Ma, I'm sorry. I'm sorry for what I said. (*He bursts into tears.*)

MA. There. There. We all say wicked things at times. I know you didn't mean it like it sounded. (*He weeps still more violently than before.*) Why, now, now! I forgive you,

Arthur, and tonight before you go to bed you . . . (*She whispers.*) You're a good boy at heart, Arthur, and we all know it. (CAROLINE *starts to cry too.* MA *is suddenly joyously alive and happy.*) Sakes alive, it's too nice a day for us all to be cryin'. Come now, get in. (*Crossing behind car to the right side, followed by the children.*) Caroline, go up in front with your father. Ma wants to sit with her beau. (CAROLINE *sits in front with her father.* MA *lets* ARTHUR *get in car ahead of her; then she closes door.*) I never saw such children. Your hot dogs are all getting wet. Now chew them fine, everybody.—All right, Elmer, forward march. (*Car starts.* CAROLINE *spits.*) Caroline, whatever are you doing?

CAROLINE. I'm spitting out the leather, Ma.

MA. Then say: Excuse me.

CAROLINE. Excuse me, please. (*She spits again.*)

MA. What's this place? Arthur, did you see the post-office?

ARTHUR. It said Laurenceville.

MA. Hhn. School kinda. Nice. I wonder what that big yellow house set back was.—Now it's beginning to be Trenton.

CAROLINE. Papa, it was near here that George Washington crossed the Delaware. It was near Trenton, Mama. He was first in war and first in peace, and first in the hearts of his countrymen.

MA (*surveying the passing world, serene and didactic*). Well, the thing I like about him best was that he never told a lie. (*The children are duly cast down. There is a pause.* ARTHUR *stands up and looks at the car ahead.*) There's a sunset for you. There's nothing like a good sunset.

ARTHUR. There's an Ohio licence in front of us. Ma, have you ever been to Ohio?

MA. No.

(*A dreamy silence descends upon them.* CAROLINE *sits closer to her father, toward the left;* ARTHUR *closer to* MA *on the right, who puts her arm round him, unsentimentally.*)

ARTHUR. Ma, what a lotta people there are in the world, Ma. There must be thousands and thousands in the United States. Ma, how many are there?

MA. I don't know. Ask your father.

ARTHUR. Pa, how many are there?

ELMER. There are a hundred and twenty-six million, Kate.

MA (*giving a pressure about* ARTHUR'*s shoulder*). And they all like to drive out in the evening with their children beside 'm. Why doesn't somebody sing something? Arthur, you're always singing something; what's the matter with you?

ARTHUR. All right. What'll we sing? (*He sketches*:)
"In the Blue Ridge Mountains of Virginia,
On the . . ."
No, I don't like that any more. Let's do:
"I been workin' on de railroad
        (CAROLINE *joins in.*)
All de liblong day.
        (MA *sings.*)
I been workin' on de railroad
        (ELMER *joins in.*)
Just to pass de time away.
Don't you hear de whistle blowin'," etc.
        (MA *suddenly jumps up with a wild cry and a large circular gesture.*)

MA. Elmer, that signpost said Camden. I saw it.

ELMER.   All right, Kate, if you're sure.

(*Much shifting of gears, backing, and jolting.*)

MA.   Yes, there it is.   Camden—five miles.   Dear old Beulah.   (*The journey continues.*)   Now, children, you be good and quiet during dinner.   She's just got out of bed after a big sorta operation, and we must all move around kinda quiet.   First you drop me and Caroline at the door and just say hello, and then you men-folk go over to the Y.M.C.A. and come back for dinner in about an hour.

CAROLINE   (*shutting her eyes and pressing her fists passionately against her nose*).   I see the first star.   Everybody make a wish.

> Star light, star bright,
> First star I seen tonight.
> I wish I may, I wish I might
> Have the wish I wish tonight.

(*Then solemnly.*)   Pins.   Mama, you say "needles".   (*She interlocks little fingers with her mother across back of seat.*)

MA.   Needles.

CAROLINE.   Shakespeare.   Ma, you say "Longfellow".

MA.   Longfellow.

CAROLINE.   Now it's a secret and I can't tell it to anybody.   Ma, you make a wish.

MA   (*with almost grim humour*).   No, I can make wishes without waiting for no star.   And I can tell my wishes right out loud too.   Do you want to hear them?

CAROLINE   (*resignedly*).   No, Ma, we know 'm already. We've heard 'm.   (*She hangs her head affectedly on her left shoulder and says with unmalicious mimicry:*)   You want me to be a good girl and you want Arthur to be honest-in-word-and-deed.

MA (*majestically*). Yes. So mind yourself. Caroline, take out that letter from Beulah in my coat pocket by you and read aloud the places I marked with red pencil.

CAROLINE (*laboriously making it out*). "*A few blocks after you pass the two big oil tanks on your left . . .*"

EVERYBODY (*pointing backward*). There they are!

CAROLINE. "*. . . you come to a corner where there's an A and P store on the left and a firehouse kittycorner to it . . .*" (*They all jubilantly identify these landmarks.*) "*. . . turn right, go two blocks, and our house is Weyerhauser St. Number 471.*"

MA. It's an even nicer street than they used to live in. And right handy to an A and P.

CAROLINE (*whispering*). Ma, it's better than our street. It's richer than our street. Ma, isn't Beulah richer than we are?

MA (*looking at her with a firm and glassy eye*). Mind yourself, Missy. I don't want to hear anybody talking about rich or not rich when I'm around. If people aren't nice I don't care how rich they are. I live in the best street in the world because my husband and children live there. (*She glares impressively at* CAROLINE *a moment to let this lesson sink in, then looks up, sees* BEULAH *off left and waves.*) There's Beulah standing on the steps lookin' for us.

> (BEULAH *enters from left, also waving. They all call out:* "Hello, Beulah—hello." *Presently they are all getting out of the car, except* ELMER, *busy with brakes.*)

BEULAH. Hello, Mama. Well, lookit how Arthur and Caroline are growing.

MA. They're bursting all their clothes.

BEULAH (*crossing in front of them and kissing her father long and affectionately*). Hello, Papa. Good old Papa. You look tired, Pa.

MA. Yes, your pa needs a rest. Thank Heaven, his vacation has come just now. We'll feed him up and let him sleep late. (ELMER *gets out of car and stands in front of it.*) Pa has a present for you, Loolie. He would go and buy it.

BEULAH. Why, Pa, you're terrible to go and buy anything for me. Isn't he terrible?

(THE STAGE MANAGER *removes automobile.*)

MA. Well, it's a secret. You can open it at dinner.

BEULAH (*puts her arm around his neck and rubs her nose against his temple*). Crazy old Pa, goin' buyin' things! It's me that ought to be buyin' things for you, Pa.

ELMER. Oh, no! There's only one Loolie in the world.

BEULAH (*whispering, as her eyes fill with tears*). Are you glad I'm still alive, Pa? (*She kisses him abruptly and goes back to the house steps.*)

ELMER. Where's Horace, Loolie?

BEULAH. He was kep' over a little at the office. He'll be here any minute. He's crazy to see you all.

MA. All right. You men go over to the Y and come back in about an hour.

BEULAH. Go straight along, Pa, you can't miss it. It just stares at yuh. (ELMER *and* ARTHUR *exit down right.*) Well, come on upstairs, Ma, and take your things.—Caroline, there's a surprise for you in the back yard.

CAROLINE. Rabbits?

BEULAH. No.

CAROLINE. Chickins?

BEULAH. No. Go and see. (CAROLINE *runs off-stage,*

down left.) There are two new puppies. You be thinking over whether you can keep one in Newark.

MA. I guess we can. (MA *and* BEULAH *turn and walk way up-stage right.* THE STAGE MANAGER *pushes out a cot from the left, and places it down left on a slant so that its foot is toward the left.* BEULAH *and* MA *come down-stage centre toward left.*) It's a nice house, Beulah. You just got a *lovely* home.

BEULAH. When I got back from the hospital, Horace had moved everything into it, and there wasn't anything for me to do.

MA. It's lovely.

(BEULAH *sits on the cot, testing the springs.*)

BEULAH. I think you'll find this comfortable, Ma.

(BEULAH *sits on down-stage end of it.*)

MA (*taking off her hat*). Oh, I could sleep on a heapa shoes, Loolie! I don't have no trouble sleepin'. (*She sits down up-stage of her.*) Now let me look at my girl. Well, well, when I last saw you, you didn't know me. You kep' saying: *When's Mama comin'? When's Mama comin'?* But the doctor sent me away.

BEULAH (*puts her head on her mother's shoulder and weeps*). It was awful, Mama. It was awful. She didn't even live a few minutes, Mama. It was awful.

MA (*in a quick, light, urgent undertone*). God thought best, dear. God thought best. We don't understand why. We just go on, honey, doin' our business. (*Then almost abruptly.*) Well, now (*stands up*), what are we giving the men to eat tonight?

BEULAH. There's a chicken in the oven.

MA. What time didya put it in?

BEULAH (*restraining her*). Aw, Ma, don't go yet. (*Taking her mother's hand and drawing her down beside her.*) I like to sit here with you this way. You always get the fidgets when we try and pet yuh, Mama.

MA (*ruefully laughing*). Yes, it's kinda foolish. I'm just an old Newark bag-a-bones. (*She glances at the backs of her hands.*)

BEULAH (*indignantly*). Why, Ma, you're good-lookin'! We always said you were good-lookin'—And besides, you're the best ma we could ever have.

MA (*uncomfortably*). Well, I hope you like me. There's nothin' like bein' liked by your family.—(*Rises.*) Now I'm going downstairs to look at the chicken. You stretch out here for a minute and shut your eyes. (*She helps* BEULAH *to a lying position.*) Have you got everything laid in for breakfast before the shops close?

BEULAH. Oh, you know! Ham and eggs.

> (*They both laugh.* MA *puts an imaginary blanket over* BEULAH.)

MA. I declare I never could understand what men see in ham and eggs. I think they're horrible.—What time did you put the chicken in?

BEULAH. Five o'clock.

MA. Well, now, you shut your eyes for ten minutes.

> (MA *turns, walks directly up-stage, then along the back wall to the right as she absent-mindedly and indistinctly sings:*)

> "There were ninety and nine that safely lay
> In the shelter of the fold . . ."

AND THE CURTAIN FALLS